Imagine That!

DEVOTIONS FOR TEENS BY TEENS

CONCORDIA PUBLISHING HOUSE · SAINT LOUIS

Library of Congress Cataloging-in-Publication Data

Imagine that! : devotions for teens by teens.

      p. cm.

   ISBN 0-7586-0379-7

  1. Christian teenagers--Prayer-books and devotions--
English. I. Concordia Publishing House.
BV4850.I49 2004
242'.63--dc22   2004000085

     5   6   7   8   9   10
16   17   18   19   20

Our Thanks to Our Teen Authors

Brendan Beale

Adam Becker

Kaysie Benedict

Brittney Billaber

Rebecca Brandt

LeAnna Christopher

Chelsea Clasen

Sarah Cusson

Faith Decker

Rebecca Dixon

Brian J. Erickson

Shaina Erwin

Mary Ettner

Willie Eustice

Elaine Filter

Brian Francis

Robbie Harris

Kristin Himmler

Alisha Hoffman

Jessica Hood

Corrie Johnson

Emily Keck

Josh Klaas

Chase Kloehn

Andrew Knipes

Hillary Kneubuhl

Mark Koschmann

Catherine Kruta

Philip Lasseigne

Josiah Laubenstein

Sarah Lemke

Laura Marine

Cameron McMasters

Christine Oberdeck

Jessica Paul

Amie Richter

Millie Rodriguez

Jessica Schafer

Rachel Schildwachter

David Schultz

Megan Sebold

Jessica Steege

Brianne Victor

Jennifer VonBergen

Beckie Walker

Kelly Warneke

Erika Wentzel

Melissa Wren

Power

Great is the LORD and most worthy of praise; His greatness no one can fathom. One generation will commend Your works to another; they will tell of Your mighty acts. They will speak of the glorious splendor of Your majesty, and I will meditate on Your wonderful works. They will tell of the power of Your awesome works, and I will proclaim Your great deeds.

Psalm 145:3-6

Making the Grade

Read: 2 Corinthians 3:4–6

Jeff had a really big biology test coming up, and weeks before the test all he did was study for that test. When the day of the test came, Jeff thought he was ready but actually he wasn't. He failed the test and was really upset with himself. The teacher came up to Jeff and asked him what happened. Jeff told him he studied forever and still did badly. The teacher asked if he had help from somebody and his answer was "No." Jeff thought he could do it by himself. When Jeff had another test a couple of weeks later, he decided to change his study habits. He asked for help studying from another student and prayed to God for help in preparing for and taking the test. Jeff's prayers and studying resulted in an "A."

2 Corinthians 3:5 says, "Not that we are competent in ourselves to claim anything for ourselves, but our competence comes from God." We cannot do everything by ourselves. Sometimes we need help. God has given us our

"reason and all our senses," our brain. Often God's help comes to us as we use what God has given us. Because of our human nature we all want to do things by ourselves. Sometimes this is impossible. Jeff got God's help when he asked for help from another student. We all need God's help.

Prayer: Dear God, we all need Your help. Even if we do not realize it, we cannot do anything without You. We are powerless apart from You. Thank You for loving us so much and being there for us, even when we do not ask. Show us ways that we can be Your helping hands to others. In Jesus' name we pray. Amen.

Getting in the Game

Read: 2 Corinthians 9:12–15

There was a water boy named Ben who wanted to be a football player. Every morning he woke up at the crack of dawn to work out. For months Ben tried and tried to get in shape and gain the weight and muscle to play football. Ben finally made it; he achieved his goal of playing football. Ben became the top running back on the team. But after his first season, Ben received a traumatizing injury and his knee was blown. He went through physical therapy and rehabilitative surgery, but his skill wasn't coming back. He didn't understand why it was taking so long to recover.

Since Ben wasn't able to practice, he had more time to spend on other projects. One of his goals was to read through the entire Bible. The more Ben read the more he began to realize that all of his gifts were from God; he hadn't done anything himself. Ben learned that there were other ways that he could serve God besides being on the football team. While Ben still gets frustrated that he can't play football as well as he used to, he has learned that God has given him a far more important gift, eternal life through the life and work of Jesus Christ. Nowadays Ben spends his time learning how he can share that message of salvation with others.

Prayer: Dear Jesus, help us to see Your will in everything we do and help us to know You make us who You want us to be. Thank You for Your gracious gift of forgiveness and eternal life through the death and resurrection of Your Son, Jesus, in whose name I pray. Amen.

Mighty Men

Read: 2 Samuel 23:8–24

David's Mighty Men! Now those guys were cool. I mean, hey, talk about power—boy did they have it. They were the top guys of the king, right? They were strong too! One guy took out 800 men in one encounter! If that's not power, then I don't know what is. Plus—that water bit? These three guys go in and take on an entire Philistine garrison just to get a drink of water for their king! Three guys against an army! The Bible is filled with stories about the amazing adventures of God's people.

Sometimes it seems like some "Mighty Men" of God is just what we need today. We face uneven odds every day. Our world can be harsh. Our everyday lives can be difficult. But we can survive the difficult times, because our God has the power.

In His Word God tells us the most incredible "power" story ever. It is the story of our Lord and Savior, Jesus. Through Jesus' perfect life,

9 (Josiah Laubenstein

death, and resurrection we receive the free gift of eternal life with Him in heaven.

God also reminds us in the Scriptures that He has not left us alone to face the day-to-day realities of life. He promises to provide for our daily needs and to defend us from evil. To paraphrase St. Paul, "If God is for us who can be against us? Not Satan, not the world, nobody can stand before the power of God." Further, 1 John 4:4 says, "You, dear children, are from God and have overcome them, because the one who is in you is greater than the one who is in the world." Now that's REAL POWER!

Prayer: Heavenly Father, we praise You for being our all-powerful God. You have given us all that we need, most importantly the gift of faith. Help us to live our lives for You. In Jesus' name. Amen.

Letting It Show Through

Read: Romans 8:28–39

Marianne was the best friend you could picture having in middle school. She never cried. She never showed any negative emotions. If it was my problem, then it was *our* problem to her. She was so strong and confident in her skin. She had that welcoming voice and those friendly eyes. We did everything together, and it seemed like there was never a moment in our lives when we weren't there for each other. In a time of need, we always pulled through for each other. I used to envision Marianne being a bridesmaid at my wedding.

Then it happened. Marianne's father died a very sudden and tragic death. It was so unexpected we didn't know how to handle it. It threw Marianne completely off track, and she ended up taking the wrong route. For a long time, the girl who could never be caught with a frown on her face was never seen with a smile. Marianne exposed the side of her personality she always hid from the world. I prayed every night for her to find peace in her father's death and within herself. Marianne came to me in tears one day saying, "Kaysie, God doesn't want me to experience this. Just take me away from it all." She handed me a slip of paper with a prayer on it. I folded it in my pocket and read it that night. It read:

> *Tell God I'm sorry for all the times I never came to Him when things were good. Please let Him know through your prayers that I desperately need something to keep me going another day.*

Of course, I let God know how she felt even though He already had her in His care. The next morning I saw the first smile from Marianne I had seen in weeks. I felt a tear roll down my cheek when she told me God had spoken to her through His Word as she studied Romans chapter 8. Her faith grew through her contact with God's Word. Marianne became again the beautiful girl she had always been on the inside and was again able to let it shine through on the outside.

Prayer: Dear Lord, let every person dealing with deep pain feel Your hand on their shoulders. Calm them with the presence of Your peace and understanding. In Your name we pray. Amen.

It's My Life!

Read: Mark 8:34–36

In the past few months I have been thinking about life a little more than usual. I'm learning more every single week. Since November, I have been playing volleyball with a girl whose mother has been diagnosed with a rare cancer. Mrs. Sumrow was diagnosed several years ago. At that time she was told that she had about three years to live after her body started a process called flushing. More than two years ago her body began this process. Mrs. Sumrow continues to undergo shots, scans, and tests to try to locate the cancer and then—if possible—treat it. So far though, the prognosis is bleak, and her health seems to be deteriorating.

Although Mrs. Sumrow's condition does not seem to be improving, she continues to stay strong. She attends practice every Sunday and Thursday, not to seek sympathy from anyone, but rather to encourage us during water breaks and to dish out high fives for everyone. This excessive optimism puzzled me. Shouldn't she be the one receiving the encouragement? To see someone without the reassurance of life tomorrow shell out this kind of support really impacted me. Shouldn't I be doing the same thing? Why doesn't God live through me like that?

The answer to the question was actually very simple; I wasn't letting God take control. It's my life, right? Wrong! Jesus says in Mark 8:34 that "if anyone would come after Me, he must deny himself and take up his cross and follow Me." My life belongs to God; He has already redeemed it when I was baptized. When I focus on me, I try to take back what is not mine. This happens to many of us. We wonder where God is in our lives, not realizing that we excluded Him from the team.

Sometimes it just takes a real life situation to help us lose the blindfolds. I've learned a lot from this experience. God is slowly helping me to know that the cross I am to bear as a Christian is to love my God and love my neighbor. Love is what Mrs. Sumrow is all about. Even if Mrs. Sumrow never gets a miracle cure, she has surely been the miracle I've needed in my life, simply through living her love.

While talking to my mother a few weeks ago about her experiences, Mrs. Sumrow told my mom, "I hope when I die my daughters can look back on this and say that their mother was brave." Even if her daughters never say it, I really want to say that I see Mrs. Sumrow as the strongest and bravest person I know. Every day she looks to God for something as simple as life. She never casts blame on Him because she knows her life is His. Mrs. Sumrow simply goes on living, and that takes true courage. She doesn't look back. She lives, and she moves on. Mrs. Sumrow faces what God gives her with faith and confidence that only God can provide. It is my prayer that God will continue to build a faith in me like hers —loving others more than myself and putting it all in His hands.

Prayer: Dear God, thank You so much for giving us this day to live for You as an opportunity to touch someone through something as simple as living. I pray that You will be with me and help me to love out loud. Grant me Your Spirit and the courage to take this step and make a difference in somebody's life today. In Your name I pray. Amen.

A Mighty God

Read: Psalm 68

Mark Koschmann

In the Old Testament the Israelites frequently came across tribes and nations who were more powerful, superior in strength and number. The enemies of the Israelites had more wealth and possessions, a stronger military, and numerous people, but sought security in false gods and idols. When Israel rested securely in the power of God they could not be intimidated by these other nations. As long as the Israelites trusted in God nothing, absolutely nothing, could stand in their way. God didn't need a huge army to protect Israel because the "earth shook, and the heavens poured down rain," before the God of Israel.

God's servant Gideon clearly illustrates the power of God described in the book of Judges (chapters 6–8). With only 300 men God delivered His people from the vast army of the Midianites and the Amalekites. In faith and trust Gideon followed his mighty and powerful God into battle, and this was certainly sufficient to ensure victory.

Where do you put your trust? Do you rest all too comfortably in the possessions and securities of this world? Talk to your Lord and Savior right now. He has the power to forgive you and to strengthen you on His path. God was victorious in the Old Testament and remains a strong and powerful God today in the 21st century. Look back on verses 34 and 35 of Psalm 68. Can you hear David's praise of our mighty God? Take time now to thank and praise the Lord our God. Then rest confidently in your Savior and in His power!

As believers we frequently pray the Lord's Prayer whether in church, Bible study, or at other fellowship events. Do you realize that this prayer clearly declares God's power and strength? At the conclusion of the Lord's Prayer, we declare our Lord's glory and power: "For Thine is the kingdom and the power and the glory forever and ever. Amen." What great words of hope, encouragement, and strength! God has the power to grant your prayers and petitions. He has all the power to strengthen you so that Satan no longer has a hold in your life. Christ Jesus demonstrated God's amazing and superior power once and for all as He rose from the dead Easter morning. Go to your Savior now in prayer and feel the power of His forgiveness at work in you right now!

Praise be to God! Amen!

Prayer: Heavenly Father, You are an awesome and powerful God! I thank You in Christ Jesus for the forgiveness of sins and life I receive in Your name. May Your Holy Spirit give me the strength to rest confidently in my Savior and in His power! Amen.

A Trial of the Unique Kind

Read: James 1:2–3, 12

(Megan Sebold)

I have never been the kind of person to enjoy running long distances. So, my sophomore year, I decided to go against everything and run cross-country. The first few weeks of practice were absolutely horrible. I got sick at the first practice and badly skinned both of my knees during a later practice. I blistered my knee in the first race. I still have scars.

Usually I would have given up and walked away from running. But something inside of me told me that I should keep on going and not give in. So I did, and it was one of the best decisions of my life. My team qualified to go to the team cross-country meet and I earned my varsity letter.

Running cross-country was one of my biggest physical trials. While our physical trials may make us frustrated, they also remind us that we live in a sin-filled world.

In his brief Epistle James reminds us that our trials in life will go beyond the physical pain that we sometimes endure. Even though we are Christians we continue to sin and suffer the results of that sin. But James also reminds us that through God's free gift of faith He has promised us the crown of life with Christ in heaven. We may endure physical and spiritual trials while on this earth, but the eternal victory has already been won for us through the life, death, and resurrection of Jesus Christ.

Prayer: Dear God, thank You for all the blessings we receive. Help us through all trials. Keep us vital and flourishing as we live each day to Your glory. Thank You, Jesus, for obtaining the victory for us and making us conquerors together with You. Amen.

Blackout

Read: John 1 2:44–46

Picture this. You're studying for finals late one spring evening. A monstrous thunderstorm is brewing outside. Lightning flashes and thunder rumbles. You are safe inside your room, or so you think. There you are minding your own business when—bam! Everything goes pitch black. You are stuck in the darkness. It is not safe to walk out of the room because you might get hurt. After a few minutes of waiting alone in the darkness, your Dad comes in with the flashlight and candles. He has rescued you from the darkness.

So it is with Jesus. We are sinful. Because of our sin, we find ourselves in the darkness of sin, alone and afraid. But God saw that we were lost and sent His one and only Son as the Light. Jesus died a horrible death on the cross to pay the price for our sin. But the story did not end there. Three days later He rose again, conquering the darkness. Christ, the Light of the World, allows us to see God the Father face-to-face in heaven through the salvation He won for us on the cross.

Prayer: Dear Lord, thank You for sending Your Son as the Light in the darkness. Now we have the assurance of seeing You face-to-face in heaven one day. In Your Son's most precious name. Amen.

Super Powers

Have you ever wished that you had "super powers"? Most kids have thought about what it would be like to have "super powers."

On the popular television show *Smallville* the main character is a teenager named Clark Kent, a.k.a. Superman. Like most teenagers Clark has to make some difficult choices and deal with complicated relationships. The problem is, Clark Kent is not like most teenagers. What makes Clark different are his "super powers." In each episode he uses his "super powers" to stop or destroy some evil that threatens the lives of others. However, Clark does have a weakness, kryptonite. When he is exposed to kryptonite it renders Clark powerless until the kryptonite is removed.

As Christians you and I have been given "super powers" through Baptism, Holy Communion, and the Word of God. These "super powers" are a gift from God to keep us strong in Christ Jesus. Like Clark Kent, these "super powers" make us different. These "super powers" also protect us when we are exposed to the evils of sin that threaten and tempt us daily.

In Baptism, we are given the "super power" of the Holy Spirit who works faith and creates in us a new "super spiritual" life. God's Word with the life-giving baptismal water works forgiveness of sins (Acts 2:38), rescues us from death and the devil (Colossians 1:13–14), and gives us eternal life (Mark 16:16).

In Holy Communion, we are given the "super power" of the true body and blood of Christ for the forgiveness of sins (Matthew 26: 26, 28). In faith, we receive Christ's words of promise that where there is forgiveness of sins there is also life and salvation (Romans 6:8–9). This "super power" is a means of grace given to us through Christ's body and blood, shed on the cross. Jesus Christ removed the kryptonite of sin from our lives so we are not rendered powerless to its effects.

The Word of God is the "super power" that guides us through life. God's Word is living and active (Hebrews 4:12). His Word shows us how God dealt with defeating the powers of hell once and for all so that we could live with Him eternally.

As we live each episode of our lives we need to remember that we have been given "super powers" that are greater than those of Clark Kent. Clark Kent is dependent upon his own "super powers" to overcome evil. His "super powers" are vulnerable and evil is never completely defeated. We on the other hand are not dependent upon our own powers but upon the "super powers" given to us by God through Jesus Christ. God has abundantly provided these "super powers" for us through Baptism, Holy Communion, and the Word of God. Jesus Christ's sacrifice for us on the cross and the empty tomb is the final episode in defeating sin and death. His "super powers" will never fail!

Prayer: Dear God, thank You for the super powerful gifts of Baptism, Communion, and Your Word. Help me to stay rooted and grounded in Christ and strengthened with the power of the Holy Spirit. Amen.

The Power of Prayer

Read: Luke 11:1–13

Prayer is a powerful thing. Being a missionary kid myself, I've seen it firsthand. I've witnessed the awesome power of our God. I've seen God work miracles—save the imperiled, cure the sick and the dying.

I lived in Thailand for a couple years when I was a little kid. My mom and dad were doing translation survey work—that is, finding out which languages need Bible translation. There was a lot of opposition, a lot of spiritual warfare going on. For many Americans, spiritual warfare is a distant topic nobody really understands. But for missionary families like mine, it is a very real fact of life.

When I was living in Thailand, I once stopped breathing in the middle of the night. There was no apparent cause, and there was nothing my parents could do—except pray. So they did, and I started breathing again. I literally wouldn't be here if it weren't for God's answer to prayer.

There was another, even more dramatic time where God saved lives. We know some missionaries who worked on an island in the Pacific. They were traveling to their island on a small boat when a violent storm blew up. Their boat was tossed back and forth, and it seemed they would never make it to land. They huddled in the back of the boat, praying to God for protection. They made it through the storm alive.

Prayer is indeed powerful—through prayer we have direct access to the merciful heart of our loving and omnipotent God. He has promised to hear and answer our prayers.

Prayer is our "Instant Messenger" service straight to God. When a Christian prays, He listens. Jesus promised that the one who asks, receives. The one who seeks, finds. And the door is opened to the one who knocks.

Prayer: Dear God, thank You for loving me and for hearing my prayers. Help me always to trust Your promises and come to You in prayer when I am in any need, fully trusting in Your grace. I pray this in Jesus' name. Amen.

Tough Times

Read: Psalm 62:8

Tears welled up in my eyes as I looked at my mom lying helpless in the Intensive Care Unit of St. Mary's Hospital. The day before she endured an intense nine-hour surgery to remove a cyst on her ovary. My dad had warned me before we entered the room that Mom might not look normal. I was naïve to think I was prepared to see her in this condition. Her skin was pale white and her lips were chapped with dry flakes. She was exhausted and could only keep her eyes open for a few seconds. An expression of confusion and frustration covered her face. I could sense she wanted to ask questions, but she was not able to speak. The doctor advised the nurses to keep her on a respirator for the day—one of the many tubes fastened to her body. There were tubes reaching in all directions and each one had a different function. There were tubes disposing of waste, blood, and discharge. Other tubes and wires regulated her heart and vital signs. My mom had no energy; she could not even breathe by herself. She was helpless.

At the same time I felt helpless. The only way I could help was to hold her hand to let her know I was there and to pray. I longed to hug my mom, but the wires, tubes, and her pain barricaded me from doing so. Within a few days she was diagnosed with ovarian cancer. The one thought recycling in my head was if cancer kills my mom, it is also killing one of my best friends.

God used this experience to teach me God's power and how to trust. I tried to help my mom in every way possible, but nothing I could ever do or say could cure the cancer. Eventually, I realized I needed to remove my pride and let God take over. Trusting God was not easy to do, but God had everything under control. By His power and love the chemotherapy treatments have been successful. Since the end of the treatments, her three-month checkups have all been good!

I have learned that trusting God in all situations is hard but it gives me peace. Knowing that God sees the big picture in every trial and that He knows what is best for me gives me great comfort. Even if my mom hadn't survived, I would have found comfort in knowing that she was in God's loving arms for all eternity.

As a baptized child of God, your heavenly Father has your life in His hands. He knows your needs, the small ones and the large ones. He knows your future and wants you to trust Him. He is an all-powerful Father. By His power He created the world. By His power He sent His Son to die for all of your sins. And by His power you can trust in Him for all things and in every situation.

Prayer: Dear Lord, You are all powerful. Thank You for always being near me in difficult times. Help me to trust in You in all situations, big and small. In Your precious name. Amen.

Without a Doubt

Read: Romans 5:1–11

Emily Keck

God gives power to each person in a different manner. Some people are physically strong and can lift cars. Others have internal strength and perseverance. My cousin, Ken, had the latter. God allowed him to be tested harder than anyone I know.

Ken was born with diabetes. He was constantly in and out of the hospital. He was confined to a wheelchair for half of his life. Ken had a beautiful daughter, but was blind and could not see her.

Ken never let his physical complications put him in a rotten mood. He was the most positive person I have ever met. He was always smiling, not a superficial smile, but an internal smile that radiated outward and spread to the people all around him. No one had better jokes than he did. He was a kind, likable person.

There was something indescribable that surrounded my cousin. It was a gift that God gives to seemingly few people. Ken could listen to my problems and make me feel better. Ken's problems were mountains compared to my sugar lumps, but he never mentioned them. Ken never made me feel inferior—he made me feel blessed.

Ken made the best of what God gave him. He always said that he wished he could do more for the people he loved. He did not know that what he gave was more than enough—for throughout his life he shared his unshakable faith in God.

When I think of the things that push me close to the edge, I feel selfish. I have never had to deal with anything compared to my cousin. When my best friend and I are fighting, when I am positive I failed my science test, when I'm overwhelmed from the hours of homework I have, when I am left numb from swim practice, and when my boyfriend hasn't called, my mom can stand up and give me a hug, and her hug reminds me that with God I can get through. He strengthens me with His Word and surrounds me with Christian friends and family who understand and encourage me. Through His Word God promises that He will watch over and strengthen me, until He calls me to my heavenly home.

Prayer: Heavenly Father, when things are tough and I'm discouraged, remind me again of Your constant love and care for me. Through Your Word help me see how Your great love extended Your arms on the cross to die for me. Show me opportunities to share Your message of love and salvation with others who have not heard. In Jesus' name. Amen.

Power Source

Read: Philippians 4:10–13

"I can do all things through Jesus Christ who strengthens me" (Philippians 4:13). The first time I read this verse I thought it meant the big things in life—the big goals that make people daring. But in the past few weeks, I have learned that God really does mean all things.

Sometime you find yourself praying for some of the dumbest things, asking the Lord to help you with the really ordinary stuff. Lately for me it has been in track practice. There are days when we have to run a mile and then two miles, while our coaches time us. Sometimes I pray for Jesus to let me use my talents and abilities to their fullest—run just one more lap, and then one more lap after that.

Another time I was in England in the middle of March. A small group from our school went on a tour. High school students were combined with college students—this proved to be a bad mixture. In England, you only have to be 18 to drink alcohol, and they aren't as strict in checking IDs as in the U.S. This set us up for a lot of peer pressure. All of the college kids were drinking; they thought I should drink to be cool like them. It wasn't hard for me to say "no." Without God's help and influence in my life, who knows what I would have done.

Things like track practice and drinking might seem little, but nothing is too great or too small for us to call upon Jesus to strengthen us. Our faith in Jesus will strengthen you for the tough times; He has given you just what you need. Be confident in who you are—a child of God; hold your head high, stay strong, and lean on Jesus. This type of strength just doesn't come from practice and training, it comes from Jesus.

Prayer: Dear God, please strengthen me to live my life the way You want me to. When things get tough give me the strength to get through. Show me Your way, through Your Word. In Your most holy name I pray. Amen.

Surviving Senior Year
(Or Moving Mountains, at the Very Least)

Read: Matthew 17:20

(Brianne Victor)

I think it is reasonable to determine that at some point in their high school career nearly every student reaches a point where they simply cannot wait for their senior year. This enthusiasm is not due to some hereditary gene that is passed down from one generation to the next, and is not bound by race, creed, or gender. It seems, rather, that there is something extra appealing about being at "the top" in the brutal society known as high school. There's supposedly a mysterious respect and confidence you acquire when you become a senior. Of course, I never fed into any of that!

Okay, so I'm lying. I was about as psyched as everyone else who entered school this year as a senior. Senior year meant carefree fun! Senior year meant special privileges! And while it does mean both these thing to a certain extent, I was not prepared for the other things that senior year meant. Senior year means applying for tens—

dare I say it—seemingly hundreds of colleges and scholarships. Senior year means being reminded about setting a good example for the underclassmen. For many of us, senior year means juggling several extracurricular activities, clubs, and challenging classes that will make us look good on the aforementioned college and scholarship applications.

Simply put, senior year is not all that it's cracked up to be (a startled gasp goes up from the audience)! It's not all fun and games. In fact, there may be times when the "fun and games" part seems nonexistent.

So what do you do now? You've been counting down the days until your blessed first day of senior year. Or maybe you're already in the thick of senior year, with 70 scholarship applications in front of your face (because let's face it, that part-time job, that major English paper, and all those after-school chores are not enough for you to handle!). Is this any reason to be filled with dread? Of course not!

Before you throw this book across the room and slump hopelessly on the couch, relax! Take a deep breath; look up. Smile, not because your dad finally fixed that stubborn leak in the ceiling, but because your heavenly Dad is watching over you. He knows your troubles, He knows your ever-growing "to do" list, and He knows you are stressing. God won't turn His back on you, because He loves and cares for you. That's His great promise!

Jesus tells us in Matthew 17:20 that with the gift of faith in God, we as mere humans can do anything! Even when we falter in our faith, which we as sinners do at every turn, the tiniest amount of faith still allows us to move mountains. Whether you're a freshman who has just begun the venture through high school, a senior who is ready to finish the venture, or somewhere in between, God loves and cares for us so very much that He will sustain you through the stress and duties that lie ahead. By faith God has blessed you with the skills you need to complete that English project, and maybe finish five or six of those college applications. Congratulations! You just moved your first mountain.

Prayer: Dear God, You know all of my burdens. You know exactly what I am going through. I know that I can do anything through faith in You. Please keep my faith strong. Keep me focused on this year and the responsibilities that I have. In Your most holy and precious Son's name I pray. Amen.

Truth

Show me Your ways, O LORD, teach me Your paths; guide me in Your truth and teach me, for You are God my Savior.

Psalm 25:4-5

Rules! What Are They Good For?

Read: Galatians 2:16

Some of you may have seen the movie *Rush Hour*. In one scene Chris and Jackie get out of a car and start singing the song, "War! What is it good for?" Every time I hear that song I always think of my friends singing their own version of the words to this Motown classic. "Rules! What are they good for? Absolutely nothing!"

As teens and young adults we sometimes wonder what rules are good for. Most of us see them as a pain or a restriction on our freedom. But think back to when you were five and your mom told you not to touch the stove. She was trying to protect you from getting hurt. Of course, you realize this now, but at the time it was just another rule.

God's rules are the same way. They are there to protect us. They are there to tell us how God wants us to live. But most importantly they are there to show us how much we need a Savior. Yet God is better than even the most loving parent. He went beyond telling us what we need to do, He provided His own Son, Jesus, to fulfill all of the rules for us. Because of our Baptism, God doesn't see our imperfect efforts to keep His Law. Instead He sees His perfect Son who perfectly kept the Law, and then died and rose again taking away the Law's punishment against us.

Prayer: God, please give me the strength to live in this world. Help me to realize Your rules are guidelines for my life. I also need help in doing Your will. Give me the wisdom to see the world's traps and to become a light in this dark world. In Jesus' name. Amen.

The New Kid

Read: Proverbs 3:5–6

Halfway through fourth grade I moved into a new school, in a new state. The first day at my new school I was afraid: afraid of the other kids, afraid of the teacher, and afraid of my new surroundings even though it was a Christian school. I cried in front of everyone. All the kids made fun of me, calling me "crybaby."

I was mad at my parents for bringing me there. I was mad at God for letting this happen to me. I wasn't myself anymore.

I thought I had one friend, but she never stuck up for me and she didn't always "feel" like hanging out with me. When it got close to the end of the year, she said the most hurtful thing to me. She said, "You know how sometimes you get bored of people? Well that's how it's getting with you. I don't think we should hang out anymore." I felt like crying but I sucked it up and pretended nothing happened. I spent the rest of that year looking for new friends.

The next year I made friends with the only two girls who would tolerate me. They were the only ones who would hang out with me, even though they didn't really like me. The other kids still made fun of me, but my "friends'" insults were more hurtful because they knew me better. I put up with this for the whole year because I didn't know what else to do.

That summer, my mom told me that I was going to go to a new school. By now I had forgiven my parents and had told my mom what was going on at school. You would think that I would want to change schools, but I didn't. "What made this school any different from the last?" I thought. I might be starting the same thing all over again. The new school would be smaller and I already knew some of the kids from church and they seemed nice. I decided to try it. Every day that summer I prayed that the kids at this school would like me. I made the decision to be myself, and I trusted that they would like me for who I am.

The first day of school the kids were really nice to me. The kids that I knew from church were really awesome. They introduced me to everyone else. Plus the teachers were really helpful. I also started sports and joined FCA (Fellowship of Christian Athletes). I found new interests and with all this came a new level of confidence.

God strengthened me through it all; I went through a lot, but I learned a lesson in being myself and being confident. I learned a more important lesson too: trust that God does everything for a reason. Now instead of running away from Him when I'm going through something hard, I pray to Him and I have the confidence to get through whatever I'm going through. When you are going through something hard, turn to God. Even if at the moment you think that God could never help you through it, He promises to be there for you. Through prayer, talk to God, He will listen and He will help. He may not do exactly what you ask, how you ask it, when you want it. But He will do what you need.

Prayer: Dear Lord, please help me with all my struggles. Help me so that even when I am going through something difficult in my life I can get through it with Your help. I also know to look for the answer in You, not in my own selfish ways. Please help me to understand this and always to look to You for help. I ask all this in Your name. Amen.

Doubts

Read: 1 Peter 1:8

Is there really a God? Do I really have faith in Him or do I just believe because my parents do? If I were to die, am I absolutely certain I would go to heaven? Do heaven and hell really exist? Did someone just make up all this stuff? Do I really need a Savior? Does God really love me, or do people just say that? Is all this "God stuff" actually the truth?

That's a list of questions I have asked myself. I guess you could sum all of it up by saying I have had many doubts. I have always been a Christian. My dad is a pastor, my mom is a Christian schoolteacher, and I have gone to Christian schools my entire life, but I question a lot. I often wish I could go back to being three or four years old and have that childlike faith that always believed without any questions.

Maybe you have felt the same way at times or have asked yourself the same questions. After every doubting phase I go through, I have come to basically the same conclusions. First, my Baptism made me a child of God, and granted me faith. Through those Baptism waters and God's Word, faith was planted in me. "And this water symbolizes Baptism that now saves you" (1 Peter 3:21). My salvation is secure with God. Second, the devil is a liar. Jesus says, "For he [the devil] is a liar and the father of lies" (John 8:44). The devil enjoys telling us "There is no God," that "You don't need a Savior," and numerous other lies. Those doubts may be the devil trying to pull you away from the truth. Third, God tells us that through faith in His Son's death and resurrection we receive eternal life in heaven as a free gift. How do we know that is the truth? Titus 1:2 says, "A faith and knowledge resting on hope of eternal life, which God, who does not lie, promised before the beginning of time." The devil lies, but God does not. His promises are true! God promises in Joshua 1:5, "I will never leave you nor forsake you." This promise holds true in times of doubt. No matter how many questions I asked, God continued to be with me and He will stay with you as well.

Lastly, "Faith is being sure of what we hope for and certain of what we do not see" (Hebrews 11:1) sums up everything. We can't see that God is there, but by faith we know He is. Even though we might ask, "How do I know I have faith?" our faith is not dependent on us. Only God can grant faith; it is a gift from Him. "For it is by grace you have been saved through faith—and this is not from yourselves—it is the gift of God" (Ephesians 2:8). Therefore, rejoice! God's plan for salvation and His Word are true!

Prayer: Dear Lord, sometimes it is hard to believe that You are there. Please grant me faith to be confident. Thank You for never leaving me and providing me with the truth in the Bible. Help me to turn to Your Word in times of doubt. Help me, Lord, to live by faith, not by sight. In Your precious name. Amen.

The Blame Game

Read: Romans 3:23

"Catherine, you need to stop talking to Aly during chapel." My religion teacher caught me by surprise as I walked into his class. I flushed, angry that I was, as I claimed, falsely accused. "But," I wanted to protest, "She talked to me first! I was trying to tell her to be quiet! It's not MY fault." But I didn't. Instead, I bowed my head, thoroughly chastised, and nodded. I realized that it was just as much my fault as Aly's. I *was* talking to her, and I definitely wasn't telling her to be quiet.

We like to blame others for our sins, don't we? If we're accused of wrongdoing, we immediately try to blame someone else. Adam did it. Eve did it. So do I. And so do you, I'm sure. We don't like to take responsibility for our actions. We make excuses and blame others so we don't get in trouble.

There's a long list of excuses people use while trying to play the Blame Game. "He hit me first!" "She made me do it!" "He started it!" "She was making me angry on purpose!" "Mom would have punished me if I had told the truth!" So many excuses, so many others to blame.

Why are we so eager to blame others for our own sins? We like to blame others because we don't like the consequences of our sin. We know what they are: punishment, disappointment, you name it. So we try to foist the blame elsewhere, to hide it from where it truly belongs. Sure, whomever you might be blaming might be just as guilty, but so are you. In fact, it's even worse now, because you're *lying* about your sin, which is just another sin to add to the pile! When you get away with blaming someone else, you'll want to do it again. It worked once, right? It could work again.

But still, there's One who knows where the true blame lies. God knows everything you do, everything you think. You can't hide the blame from God, so trying is useless. We don't want to admit we're wrong. But it is possible. Through God's Law we see our sin and we are moved to repent.

The best part of all—when we fess up to sinning—God forgives us. And then He forgets we've ever sinned. Because of His forgiveness we're a new person in His eyes, acceptable in the kingdom of heaven. So, why try to blame someone else for our sins, when we can confess, repent, and receive *that*?

Prayer: Heavenly Father, forgive me for the times I've blamed others instead of admitting my own sin. Give me strength to follow You in times of temptation. In the name of Christ Jesus my Savior. Amen.

The Full Story

Read: Colossians 2:9–10

(Sarah Cusson)

Do you sometimes wonder where you are most complete, where you find your identity? What makes you complete? Do you find your identity in the sports you play, the people you hang out with, or your own individual talents? The dictionary defines identity as "individuality." What makes you an individual?

The dictionary also defines identity as the state of being identical. God's Word defines our identity in relationship to Christ, "For you died, and your life is hidden with Christ in God" (Colossians 3:3). Who are you? Jesus Christ made you His child through your Baptism. He gives you an identity and a life that is identical to His. "It is because of Him [God] that you are in Jesus Christ, who has become for us wisdom from God—that is, our righteousness, holiness, and redemption" (1 Corinthians 1:30).

I know you may be thinking, "Hello, we're in the real world. I know Jesus gives me fullness and 'stuff,' but I really have trouble finding my identity in Him. I want to, but it just doesn't work in this life." But the truth is the Lord will not leave you alone. He promises to give you strength ("He will keep you strong to the end . . ." *1 Corinthians 1:8a*) and will always be with you ("And surely I am with you always, to the very end of the age" *Matthew 28:20b*). This world is not easy; the devil provides many opportunities for us to stumble and fall. But God has placed His Spirit within us as a deposit guaranteeing what is to come (see 2 Corinthians 1:21–22). God sent His only Son, Jesus Christ, to die and rise so that you might be redeemed by His blood. Now when God looks at you, all He sees is the blood of Jesus that covers you. 1 John 3:1 says, "How great is the love the Father has lavished on us, that we should be called children of God! And that is what we are!" You have an identity as a child of God. Through the hard times in our lives we can trust the Lord to provide for all our needs. He will strengthen us through His Word and Holy Communion. All other things will pass away, but the Lord and His Word will never pass away (Matthew 24:25).

Prayer: Dear Lord Jesus, thank You for loving me. Help me always remember that my true identity is in You as Your Child. In Your precious name I pray. Amen.

Never Forsaken

Read: Psalm 139:7–16

Wilmer McLean, a retired major in the Virginia militia, was farming in northern Virginia. The Battle of First Manassas (also called the First Battle of Bull Run), fought during the Civil War, occurred on Wil's farm. Concerned for his family's safety, Wil moved his family to Charlottesville before the fighting began. But the war followed him there. Wounded from First Manassas and other battles around the area poured in. Wil McLean moved his family once again to a quiet town in central Virginia called Appomattox. But the war managed to find him there too. On April 9, 1865 Generals Robert E. Lee and Ulysses S. Grant would meet in Wil McLean's home to establish the conditions for the surrender of the Confederate army, bringing about the end of the war. Historians have quipped that the Civil War began in Wil McLean's front yard, and ended in his parlor. The man who tried everything to get away from the war ended up being host of the surrender party.

We are a lot like Wil McLean. We mess up time and time again. Instead of going to God with repentant hearts we try to "fix" it ourselves. We do everything to try and run from our sin. But God never gives up on us. St. Paul reminds us, "For I am convinced that neither death nor life, neither angels nor demons neither the present nor the future, nor any powers, neither height nor depth, nor anything else in all creation will be able to separate us from the love of God that is in Christ Jesus our Lord" (Romans 8:38–39). No matter what you do, no matter where you go, God will never forsake you—He will never forget you. Even when we have done something so bad we wonder if God can forgive, He is there with His mercy and grace. God sent us His only Son, Jesus Christ, to pay the price for our sin on the cross at Calvary. Through His free gift of faith we receive the promise of eternal life with Him.

Prayer: Dear Lord, thank You so much for being with me this day and every day. I pray that You will grant me a heart that desires only You and Your Word. Help me to follow You every day. In Jesus' name. Amen.

Stressed Out

Read: Romans 8:35

7:30 P.M. Sunday and you are doing homework. You have been doing homework almost all weekend. You did some before you went to the basketball game on Friday. Saturday, you went to work at 9:30 A.M. You did some homework there, but not enough. You left work at 1:30 P.M. and when you got home you did some more. Now it is Sunday and you are still trying to finish all your homework.

It's just as bad during the week. You start school at 8:30 and get out at 3:00. At school you listen to teachers lecture and assign more homework than you have time for. This happens five days in a row.

When you get home from school, you have things that need to be done. You have to finish your homework for the next day. It could take three to four hours to complete it all. There are a few days that you are scheduled to work. You have appointments and other things. You need to get some exercise. All this sitting and doing homework isn't healthy. If you are an athlete, you have practice after school. All you know is that something needs to be cut out of your schedule.

Sadly, most of the time, God gets cut out of your day. Rather than spending time with God we focus on homework, jobs, appointments, and athletics.

God gives us the strength to manage all the stress that school and after school activities bring. You can go to Him for strength and relaxation. He loves and cares for us. God showed His love by sending His Son, Jesus, to earth. Jesus Christ died on the cross to take away all of our sins. In His Word, God promises to hear our prayers and provide all that we need for this life and the next.

Prayer: Dear heavenly Father, I trust you to relieve the stress in my life. Help me to spend more time with You. I know that life is not easy and that I do leave You out of it sometimes. Be with me through all the stress and tough times. In Your precious name I pray. Amen.

Life's Not Fair

Read: John 14:27

(David Schultz

James is always getting good grades, yet he barely studies. I have to study for hours just to get a decent grade. Thomas is awesome at sports, and he doesn't even have to practice; it just comes naturally for him. I have to practice all the time and I am still nowhere close to being as good as the other guys in my class. Derek is "Mr. Popular"; he has tons of friends while I have only a few.

Does this sound familiar? Do you ever feel left out, put down, or all alone? Does life seem unfair? Well the answer is—YES! Life is not fair at all! There are plenty of horrible, unfair things that happen in this world. People we know and love die. Family and friends get sick. Terrorists attack our nation and make us feel unsafe. There are tragic things that happen in our country every day, and we wonder why. Why do these things happen to us?

The answer of course is sin. Since the fall into sin our world has been tainted by its stain. The good news is that Jesus is with us even when life is not fair. He helps us when we struggle, or when we feel life is unbearable. Jesus suffered on the cross to take our sins on Himself. He suffered, died, and rose again to save us. It wasn't fair that He had to die for our sins, He did it because He loves us. Forgiven by Him, given the gift of His Word and Sacraments, we find a source of strength that helps us carry through even the toughest times.

Prayer: Dear heavenly Father, help me and strengthen me when life just isn't fair, so I realize that You are with me. I am never alone. In Jesus' name I pray. Amen.

Love

I will praise You, O Lord my God, with all my heart; I will glorify Your name forever. For great is Your love toward me; You have delivered me from the depths of the grave. You, O Lord, are a compassionate and gracious God, slow to anger, abounding in love and faithfulness.

Psalm 86:12-13, 15

Don't Be Self-Reliant

Read: 1 John 4:13–18

A homeless man named Joe wandered into my church one day. The people in the congregation welcomed him, and he started attending regularly. Very soon Joe got a job through the efforts of a member of the church. After a couple of years Joe was able to buy a house for himself. Joe's blessings came when the Holy Spirit caused him to rely on God. What a cause for celebration!

We are all in some way like the homeless man. We don't listen to others or want help from others. God, through His Word, causes us to turn to Him and recognize Him as the source of everything we need. 1 John 4:15–16 puts it this way, "If anyone acknowledges that Jesus is the Son of God, God lives in him and he in God. And so we know and rely on the love God has for us." Because of His love given for us through the work of Christ on the cross of Calvary we learn to share His love with others.

Prayer: Dear God, thank You for the love You show us through Jesus Christ, given as our Savior from sin. Help us recognize You as the source of the many blessings we receive. Help us to rely upon You and not on ourselves. Encourage us to reach out to those who don't know You. In Your name we pray. Amen.

Hope

Read: Psalm 71:1–6

Growing up is hard today. The devil and the world want to lead us away from our goals and dreams. The messages we hear pull us in many different ways. We try to stay away from drugs and alcohol. Our parents went from being our comfort to our enemies. We try hard to not cuss and swear. Society tells us that sex is okay in almost all circumstances. We try to keep up with classes and homework. We foolishly say to ourselves, "Homework just gets in the way of the weekend. I'll do it on Monday." Suicide might be the best road. Religion is for nerds. Discussing faith is to be avoided.

Life as a Christian teen can be risky. Sometimes you feel alone and hated. You don't fit in and you blame yourself and God. It seems hard to form close friendships. It seems like a long time since we felt close to God.

But when we feel far away from God, He is still right there by our side. God promises in His

Word that He will never leave us alone to face by ourselves the trials that the world puts in our way. In fact, God sends His own Spirit to live in us so that we can always rely on Him instead of just ourselves.

In addition God gives us the opportunity to gather with other believers on a regular basis as we come together for worship, the Lord's Supper, Bible study, and youth group. As we gather with other believers God strengthens us to face the rest of the world. He provides these opportunities to gather with others who share our faith as a way to reassure us that we are not alone in our faith walk. God uses Word and Sacrament and fellow believers to share His love with us, and then He uses us to share His love with others.

Prayer: Dear Lord, be my refuge, be my shield, be the weapon of hope that I wield. And when those days come, the ones I don't like, let me remember that You gave me life. Amen.

The Waiting Room

Read: Luke 10:27

When I was about four years old I started having a lot of bruising all over my body. Some bruises were in the shape of handprints where I had been touched or where one of my friends had grabbed me to pull me over to look at something. My parents noticed this and took me to the doctor. The doctor said I either had Immune Thrombocytopenic Purpura (ITP), a rare blood disease where your body kills off the platelets in your blood allowing free bleeding, or leukemia, a deadly form of cancer. The doctor said we would have to go to the hospital and have blood work done.

You can imagine my parents' distress and concern while waiting for the blood work to be done and tested. There was a chance that their little girl could die. Another couple in the hospital noticed my parents' distress and came over and talked with them for a while. My parents told them about our situation and the couple consoled, comforted, and showed love to my parents. Come to find out, their son who was five years old, had been diagnosed with leukemia and was dying. Yet these people forgot about their troubles to comfort my parents. When the blood work came back, the results showed that I had ITP. Thankfully, ITP is a very rare condition that occurs only once in a person's life, in a minute percentage of children. After a period of time, childhood ITP and its symptoms disappear completely. The doctors expected me to make a complete recovery. The couple found out and congratulated my mom and dad and showed such generous compassion to people they had never met before.

More than ten years have passed and my bout with ITP is nothing but a distant memory. In Luke 10:27 it says, "'Love the Lord your God with all your heart and with all your soul and with all your strength and with all your mind' and, 'Love your neighbor as yourself.'" The couple at the hospital did exactly that for my family. They showed their love to their neighbors—my parents. They truly set an example of faith that my parents and I will never forget. They forgot their own pain and showed love to someone else who needed it.

But because of our sin we can never keep this command perfectly, so God did the greatest thing for us. He showed us love by sending His only Son to die on the cross for us, to forgive our sins, so that we could live with Him for all eternity. God gives us His Spirit to strengthen our faith and to help us share the message of His love and salvation with others.

Prayer: Dear Lord, please remind us each and every day of the love You showed to us by sending Your Son, Jesus Christ, to die on the cross for us. Help us to show love to one another and live a Christlike life. Be with those who need Your love and need to learn of Your love. In Jesus' name. Amen.

Teens in Bondage

Read: Galatians 4:3–7

"So also, when we were children, we were in slavery under the basic principles of the world." (Galatians 4:3)

So they *finally* admit it! Teens *are* treated as slaves! We are born and then used for hard labor, right . . . ?

Well, believe me, when I first read this verse, I was mad. It made me feel so unimportant. How could a God so loving, wise, and awesome betray me by making me a slave?

Now I obviously was overreacting, so after I cooled down I did a little research. I read Paul's words to the church in Rome. "But now that you have been set free from sin and have become slaves to God, the benefit you reap leads to holiness, and the result is eternal life" (Romans 6:22). In fact God has made us His heirs of salvation (Galatians 4:7).

Why did I act so ignorant before? Of course I'm a slave—and I want everyone to know my Master. Now instead of being a slave to the world, I'm free to be a slave to my Lord, Jesus Christ. I'm forgiven. Thank You, Jesus!

Prayer: Dear Lord, I read these passages and I hear Your Word, but I pray that I will truly understand it and put it into practice. Thank You so much for the things I notice daily, as well as for the things that make the smallest difference, but I never seem to see. Thank You for Your unlimited forgiveness and mercy. Keep me always in Your light, reaching out to others to know You also. You are my Lord and Savior and I am eternally grateful. Amen.

Stood Up

(Jennifer VonBergen)

Read: Proverbs 3:5–6

Saturday was a whirlwind of activities. I woke up early to attend a cross-country meet, ran like lightning, and drove home to get ready to attend my first Homecoming dance. I was ecstatic. I thought nothing could burst the joy and excitement I felt.

My parents had purchased my first formal dress, a beautiful blue with matching shoes, after my boyfriend, Stephen, asked me to the dance. I was thrilled to have a nice, Christian young man to attend the dance with. Stephen and I planned to meet at the dance because of the transportation logistics. My parents took pictures at home and planned on taking pictures of the two of us before the dance. I even arrived at school early despite the frenzy of excitement over going to my first dance with a guy.

Six o'clock came and went. I was sure Stephen was just running a little late. He would certainly be there. I stood outside patiently waiting. I knew he wouldn't let me down. My parents waited with me for an hour. Seven o'clock—coronation started and finished, but still no sign of Stephen. Finally, at eight o'clock, a half hour after the dance started, he came into the dance—with another girl! I was hurt and angry. I couldn't believe that Stephen had stood me up!

Thankfully, God doesn't cheat and lie to His children. He is always there caring for us. Even though I felt alone, humiliated, and unloved, God was there with me. Proverbs reminds us, "Trust in the LORD with all your heart and lean not on your own understanding; in all your ways acknowledge Him and He will make your paths straight" (Proverbs 3:5–6). God's eternal love, demonstrated on the cross at Calvary, will never diminish no matter how often we sin and turn away from Him.

It has been hard to forgive my now ex-boyfriend, but I have managed to do so. I know that God strengthened me through His Spirit and enabled me to forgive Stephen. God gives me this strength through His Word and Holy Communion. I thank God for His everlasting care of me.

Prayer: Dear Lord God, I thank You for the many blessings and talents You have given to me. Help me live like Your child, forgiving and loving my enemies and others who do wrong to me. I know that I am not perfect and I need the forgiveness that only You can give. Please grant me Your mercy. In the name of Jesus. Amen.

A Father's Love

(Christine Oberdeck

Read: 1 John 4:10

One Sunday morning I woke up extremely stressed. That whole weekend had been a disaster. The last thing I wanted to do was go to church. Even though spending time with my Lord and Savior would have been the best thing for me to do, I didn't go to church that morning. My dad had already left for church by the time I got up; my mom just went by herself. As the morning went on I dreaded seeing my dad when he came home. I knew he wouldn't be happy that I skipped church. I was right. He came in the door and asked, "Were you there today?" I replied with a simple "No." I could see the disappointment in his face, but that was the end of the discussion. I felt horrible. I had disappointed my dad and God for that matter.

Later that day, I walked past the bathroom and saw my dad cleaning. That was my job! I was supposed to clean the bathrooms. I deserved to do the dirty work. I wanted to clean the bathrooms to pay for what I had done that morning. However, my dad took it upon himself. My dad did the work I was supposed to do!

My heavenly Father did the same thing. I can't follow God's law perfectly. I sin every day. Because of my sin and failure to follow the Law, I deserve to die and be separated from God forever. However, my heavenly Father has immense love and compassion. He sent His only Son, Jesus Christ, to do the dirty work for me. Jesus didn't clean my bathroom, but He cleaned my soul. His death wiped away all the grime and mildew of my sin. Jesus' righteous blood cleanses me and makes my sins "whiter than snow" (Isaiah 1:18).

We deserve to die; "the wages of sin is death" (Ephesians 2:8). However, our Father in heaven lavished His love on us through His Son's death and resurrection. Out of love my dad cleaned the bathrooms. How much greater is the love of our heavenly Father who cleans our souls and gives us the free gift of eternal life!

Prayer: Dear Lord, You have so much fatherly love, it's hard to comprehend. You sent Your only Son to die and do the dirty work to pay for my sins. Please forgive me of my sins and help me to share Your amazing love each and every day with those around me. In Your precious name. Amen.

I'm Just a Phone Call Away

Read: Psalm 17:6–7

"I'm just a phone call away." These were my best friend's parting words as she moved a few years ago. Having my best friend living so far away is hard. But we realize that we have a strong friendship. No matter how far apart we are, we are friends, and we are not going to lose contact. My best friend and I stay in touch over the phone on a regular basis. You have to work to keep that friendship going, and growing stronger. Even if you can't see your best friend every day of your life, it doesn't mean that you can't be close to them.

God is always there for you to talk to even though we cannot see Him face-to-face. Some people say they can't see God so therefore He doesn't understand what's going on in our lives. Yet, God is closer than a phone call. You don't even have to pick up a phone, and our God listens. Even when things don't always come out the way you like them, it doesn't mean that He doesn't listen and care. He talks to us daily as we read His holy Word. God promises to always hear and answer our prayers.

Prayer: Lord, be with us as we go through our day. Guide us and let us know that You are there for us always and forever. Be with all who don't believe in You, and help us to share Your message of love with them. Help us during our troubled times; reassure us of Your great love. Thank You, Lord, for all You have done for us. We love You, Lord. In Your name we pray. Amen.

Chosen with Love

(Brian J. Erickson)

Read: John 15:16

I am blessed to have been raised in a Christian family who faithfully brought me up in the church and instilled in me Christian values. Unfortunately sometimes I tend to become too confident of my own "goodness." Because I have always had the church in my life, I tend to take my faith for granted. I begin to think I can take care of myself. Hey, if I go to church every weekend I must be on good terms with God, right?

Those of us who don't know any other lifestyle besides the Christian lifestyle sometimes forget what a friend we have in Jesus. He continues to do amazing things in our lives. Our very lives are amazing signs of God's gracious love! We have been created in His image. We have been given amazing talents and abilities, a conscience and a free will informed by faith to make our own decisions. Unfortunately, we abuse these gifts. We don't always allow our conscience to help us decide what's right from wrong. Even when we know something is wrong, we do it anyway, perhaps because it brings a false sense of joy and happiness or fulfills our fantasies.

John 15:16 reminds us of how very special we are to God. We don't have to go on a wild chase to find God. He came looking for us. He created us, He loves us, and He has graciously given us His forgiveness, grace, and salvation. He is always there for us, even in times when He seems so far away, the painful times when it seems there is no hope—He is right there beside us, reaching out with open arms to comfort and console us.

Prayer: Lord, You are so amazing. Your love and grace is ever flowing. We continue to separate ourselves from Your gracious love in an attempt to be self-sufficient and independent. Help us always to do everything according to Your will, for Your glory. Help us to come to you not only in times of trial, but in times of joy. Help us to recognize Your intense love for us, a love that led to the cross, a cross that did not bring death, but eternal life. When we feel we are not deserving of Your love because of our sin, help us to admit our brokenness and need for Your mercy. Help us to live in that forgiveness, so that we may live each day to the fullest, enjoying Your creation, and one day, Your eternal kingdom. Amen.

Guilty, as Charged!

Read: John 3:16–17

Remember doing something you felt so guilty about—so ashamed of. You know you shouldn't have done it, but you did it and now it's over. You die inside, dreading that your Mom and Dad will surely find out. They come home and it's written all over your face. They don't even have to ask; they can already tell something is wrong and you had everything in the world to do with it.

You escape to your room to hide the guilt. Soon Mom comes in and makes it very clear: she does not like what you did, but she still likes you, even loves you. As she gives you a big hug and holds you tight, you have that wonderful, warm feeling of knowing LOVE and being LOVED. You have the assurance that everything is going to be all right. This is unconditional love.

How much more wonderful is our heavenly Father's unconditional love for us! "This is how God showed His love among us: He sent His one and only Son that we might live through Him" (1 John 4:9). This is the greatest demonstration that shows God's love for us. It is real love, not that we loved God, but that He loved us; sending His Son as a personal atonement or payment for our sins. Our faith moves us to share this wonderful fact. God loves us so much that He is willing to forgive us. He sent His Son to die for us. We are so undeserving of His unconditional love, yet because of His grace we have eternal life. "For it is by grace you have been saved . . . it is the gift of God . . ." (Ephesians 2:8).

God's love and faithfulness is unfailing, nothing can separate us from Him.

In our worship, we confess our sins and receive comfort in the words of the Absolution spoken by our pastor. "Praise be to the God and Father of our Lord Jesus Christ who has blessed us . . . For He chose us . . . In Him we have redemption through His blood, the forgiveness of sins, in accordance with the riches of God's grace . . ." (Ephesians 1:3–8).

Prayer: Dear heavenly Father, I pray for Your unfailing grace and forgiveness. I am so undeserving, and yet You have sent Your Son to pay for my sins. Guide me with Your Word and give me the courage to speak of Your forgiveness and grace to others. Help me to share Your unconditional love with others. In Jesus' name I pray. Amen.

Wouldn't It Be Easier?

Read: Colossians 1:21–23

(Jessica Schafer

Sometimes I feel like it would be easier if I didn't believe in God. My life would go along a lot smoother if God weren't in my life. I wouldn't feel bad for doing something I know I shouldn't do. I just wouldn't feel the pressure to be good all the time. I see people who don't have God in their lives, and they just seem happier, because they don't have to feel bad about things.

But I know that they just *seem* not to have a care in the world. I realize that this is just the devil's way of trying to distract me from God. I know that I can't act the way I should all the time. I can never be perfect in what I do. I will always mess up my life some way or another. But because I mess up is why God steps in. The blood of Jesus, shed on the cross, covers my mistakes and sins. My lack of perfection is covered by His perfect life, death, and resurrection.

Jesus reminds us in His Word: "I have said this to you, so that in Me you may have peace. In the world you will face persecution. But take courage; I have conquered the world!" (John 16:33). No matter what challenges I face in life, I won't have to worry about anything: "But God proves His love for us in that while we still were sinners Christ died for us" (Romans 5:8). God took care of everything for us when He sent His Son to die for us.

No matter what we go through in life, it is nothing when compared to what Christ had to go through on the cross for us. I thank God every day, knowing that while I'm not perfect, He loves me anyway. Yes, we are sinners who deserve nothing more than punishment for the sins we have committed, but no matter how much we deserve punishment God gives us love right back. He loves us and He makes that love real every day through the people He puts in our lives, our family and friends who mean so much to us.

Prayer: Dear Lord, I pray that You will continue to love me, no matter what I do. Forgive my sins, for I deserve nothing but punishment. I pray You, help me to never forget how much You love me and how special we all are to You. Lord I pray that You would be with me most of all when I feel like my life doesn't matter. Show me that I have a purpose, a meaning for being here. I know that You have a plan for all of us. Help me to see Your plan for me. In Your most precious name. Amen.

He Will Never Leave You

Jessica Steege

Read: Deuteronomy 31:6;
Romans 8:39

"Why is this happening to me?" This question is often asked when people have something bad happen in their life. I have asked God this question over and over again throughout the course of my life. I don't know if I have ever really received an answer, but I trust that God knows best.

When I was four years old, I lost my only sister to asthma. There was quite an age difference, she was almost sixteen, but we had a special relationship that made the age difference unnoticeable. The day I came home to find out my sister had died was the hardest day of my life. Since I was only four, I had no idea what death even was; my parents had to explain it to me. My mom remembers that I had tears coming down my cheeks and said, "Does this mean I don't have a sister anymore?"

Going to school only made things worse; there was no one who could understand what I was going through. It hurt to see my classmates complain about their siblings; it was just a reminder that I no longer had my sister. Whether they were kidding around or fighting, at least they had each other. I would have given anything to have what they had, but I knew that I would never be able to. I felt alone and was mad at God for taking away my best friend.

I honestly don't know exactly when I stopped being mad at God for my loss, but over time I began to accept the fact that she was gone. I even began to understand that God had a plan for her life just as He has a plan for mine. She is already safely in His arms for all eternity.

It has been almost thirteen years since my sister died. I still have my sad moments from time to time, usually when I think back to all the good memories I had with my sister. I still think of her whenever I hear her favorite song or smell her perfume. I know that she will not be there for my graduation or my wedding. Tears fill my eyes when I think of all the memories we could have had together. But I know God will get me through it.

I now look for the good that God planned to come from this tragic event. I believe that my experiences have allowed me to relate to others who have lost a loved one, especially if it is recent and they are really struggling. Sometimes people just need a shoulder to cry on: the shoulder of someone who understands what they are going through.

I pray daily to become stronger in my faith and closer to God. In His Word God has promised me that He will never leave me alone; He will never forsake me. One day God will come to take me to my home in heaven where I will share in the joy that my sister already knows.

Prayer: Dear Lord, I pray for all who have lost a loved one and who wonder if they will ever be happy again. Comfort them and let them know they are not alone. Give them peace and hope, so that they trust the promise of eternal life with You in heaven. Let them know You have a plan, and although they may not understand exactly what it is, give them the understanding that You know best. Help them to know You love them and will get them through. Let them know that You will always be there, no matter what. Amen.

Praise

Praise the LORD, O my soul; all my inmost being, praise His holy name. Praise the LORD, O my soul, and forget not all His benefits—who forgives all your sins and heals all your diseases, who redeems your life from the pit and crowns you with love and compassion, who satisfies your desires with good things.

Psalm 103:1-5a

Lost and Found

(Brian J. Erickson)

Read: Luke 19:9–10

I watch as one of my best friends walks up to the front of the sanctuary. It is her turn to give her testimonial. Six months of hard work and classes with the goal of becoming a peer minister are coming to a conclusion as seven of my peers and I prepare to be commissioned into service as peer ministers. Sadly enough each of us knows that our friend, who is about to give her testimonial, will be leaving us soon to move to Colorado.

She stands at the front of the sanctuary with tears already forming in her eyes. She begins explaining how her family had never gone to church or encouraged her to attend church. Her first experience with our congregation had come when she joined one of her friends for a youth event. Slowly but surely she began to attend more and more youth events with our group. Eventually, she began to also attend worship services as often as possible. Her eyes begin to fill with tears. She begins to confess what an amazing impact God has had on her life. Tears of joy stream down her face as she proclaims what an amazing God we have, who has done such wonderful things in her life and has changed her in beautiful ways. Not only has God given her a reason to look forward to each day but He has also given her amazing friends who share her beliefs and values, and on whom she can lean in times of trouble and pain. Although she is deeply struck with grief because she is leaving these people she loves so much, she knows she can trust the Lord.

As I sat in that sanctuary and watched a young woman proclaim what an amazing friend she had in Jesus, I realized how amazing God really is. I know I take His love, grace, and forgiveness for granted. I sometimes stray from the path He has set in front of me. I don't understand how I can stray from a God who not only can call His children to Himself from non-Christian families, but who also gave His life on a cross for my salvation. Yes, what an amazing grace we have received! God sent His only Son into the world to live and die and rise again so that He can give me the free gift of eternal life.

Prayer: Lord God, thank You for the free gift of salvation through faith in Jesus Christ. Help me to grow in my faith day by day. Strengthen my faith as I come to the Lord's Table to receive Your very body and blood in Holy Communion. Use this gift to strengthen me in my daily walk with You. Help me to share the joy I find in You with my non-Christian friends and their families. In Jesus' name I pray. Amen.

It Doesn't Make Sense

Read: Isaiah 55:8–9

It didn't make sense—but God told Noah to build an ark, . . .

> *Noah did everything just as God commanded him . . . For forty days the flood kept coming on the earth, and as the waters increased they lifted the ark high above the earth. The waters rose and increased greatly on the earth, and the ark floated on the surface of the water . . . Every living thing on the face of the earth was wiped out; men and animals and the creatures that move along the ground and the birds of the air were wiped out from the earth. Only Noah was left and those with him in the ark.* Genesis 6:22; 7:17–18, 23

Noah and his family were saved by God, passing through the same waters that destroyed everything else.

It doesn't make sense. Why does school have to be stressful, why do parents have to get a divorce, why do friends die, why do people we know have to go to war, why do parents lose jobs, and why does the future have to be so uncertain, but . . .

> *We rejoice in our sufferings, because we know that suffering produces perseverance; perseverance, character; character, hope. And hope does not disappoint us, because God has poured out His love into our hearts by the Holy Spirit, whom He has given us.* Romans 5:3–5

God gives us comfort and helps us grow from these experiences.

It doesn't make sense that bread and wine are the body and the blood, but . . .

> *Jesus took bread, gave thanks and broke it, and gave it to His disciples, saying, "Take and eat; this is My body." Then He took the cup, gave thanks and offered it to them saying, "Drink from it all of you. This is My blood of the covenant, which is poured out for many for the forgiveness of sins.* Matthew 26:26–28

It's a gift from God that gives us forgiveness of sins.

It doesn't make sense that God uses us, sinful people, to tell others about Christ and His saving grace, but . . .

> *I can do everything through Him who gives me strength.* Philippians 4:13

God gives us strength, wisdom, and the Holy Spirit to assist us and help us. He equips us.

It doesn't make sense that the Father would give up His only innocent Son and let Him be beaten, bruised, laughed at, nailed to a tree, and die but . . .

God so loved the world that He gave His one and only Son, that whoever believes in Him shall not perish but have eternal life. John 3:16

God the Father gave up His Son, Jesus, to pay for all of our sins, each and every one. He didn't deserve to die, but He paid the ransom so that through faith we may go to heaven and live with our Savior forever.

It doesn't make sense; we should have been the ones to die eternally, but let's be thankful that some things just don't make sense.

Prayer: Lord, some things just don't make sense. At the same time You are taking care of me and using me as You want to. You have everything under control. It doesn't make sense that Jesus came to die for me, but He did. Thank You, Lord, for Your saving grace and that some things just don't make sense. In Your precious name. Amen.

How Am I Praising God?

Read: Psalm 8

Do I honor God with the things that I say, with the things I watch on television, with the clothes that I wear, and with the way that I act? Is the music I listen to pleasing to God? Do I praise God with the way I live my life? Can people who don't know me tell that I am a Christian by the way I live my life?

These are some tough questions. Sadly, the answer for most of us is a resounding "No!" It's hard growing up, going to school, trying to live the way you know honors God—the way He wants us to live that gives all the glory to Him. The way we live declares we are enemies of God. Yet God, through Jesus Christ, has already covered over my failings and sin.

When we go to church on Sunday and hear the words, "Given and shed for you for the remission of sins," I'm overjoyed that we are so blessed to have the assurance that Jesus paid with His life for our sins to be forgiven. And it's not just the "big" sins, but sins that we often overlook. Remember that there are no "little" or "big" sins, in God's eyes, they are all SINS, for which He freely offers His forgiveness. I don't have to spend time asking myself, "Should I have done that? Should I have said that? Did I take advantage of my opportunities to spread God's love?"

Because we are baptized, we live under God's forgiving grace. His Spirit moves us to praise God with the talents He gave us and with the understanding that He is the ultimate reason to lift up your voice, sing, dance, and shout to the Lord!

Through faith you can let others see your light shine; let others see how wonderful our Father's love truly is. Trust that your gifts will be a witness to those around you, people who are non-Christian or are Christians who do not recognize His amazing works. Share your experiences of God's grace and mercy with others. I love coming back after a youth gathering and sharing with my friends what a great time I had singing, having fun, and praising our awesome God. It gives me chills to look out and see 35,000 other teens who are just like me. It is an indescribable feeling that rushes through your body to see the magnitude of His Love.

Prayer: Dear God, You are truly our awesome God. Help me to use every opportunity to sing Your praises and lift up Your name. Continue to bless me with the gifts You have graciously given to me and help me to use these gifts to reach out to others. In Jesus' name I pray. Amen.

Close Calls

Read: Psalm 91:11–12;
Matthew 28:20b

I know God loves us and protects us. You see, my family has had a strange number of close calls that could only have been survived through God's loving care of us. There have been close calls with near drowning. One time my cousin saved me; another time I saved a younger cousin and her sister.

The most memorable time was one day when my cousin and I high-centered our ATV on a sand dune. We were stuck in the desert's summer heat for an hour and a half. Just then, a military jet flew right over us. At first it made things worse because the jet was so low the heat from the exhaust was unbearable. However, the sight of the jet made a group of people, a couple hundred yards away, look over and see us flagging them down for help.

My family has witnessed many examples of God's love and compassion. In His Word God reassures us that even His holy angels watch over us. At the end of the Gospel of Matthew Jesus tells His followers, and us, of His continuing care for all of His followers. Most importantly, God gives us saving faith. Through faith, when our life here on earth is done, He brings us to our eternal rest with Himself in heaven.

Prayer: Lord, You care for us every day of our lives. Help us to recognize Your daily care and concern for us all. Continue to strengthen us through Your Holy Word. In Jesus' name. Amen.

Day of Trouble

Read: Matthew 11:28–30;
Psalm 50:15

It seems "day of trouble" could easily describe the typical teenager's life. Troubles with friends; troubles with homework; troubles with sports, music, after-school activities; troubles with teachers; troubles with parents and siblings; at times the list seems endless. The troubles of life leave us feeling stressed and more than a little out of control.

With all the concerns and worries of today, it is easy to lose sight of the Lord and become engulfed in our own problems. It becomes easy to forget that we can call upon our God in our troubles and find comfort, peace, and hope. In Matthew Jesus tells us that He will take care of our troubles, no matter how many or how heavy they may be. Whatever burden(s) we are carrying, He has taken them upon Himself. The weight will be lifted from our shoulders and onto His through His grace and love for us.

We have this assurance from God. We are reminded through our Baptism that we are forgiven and made

(LeAnna Christopher

new each day through the forgiveness of sin. Yet we continue to dwell on the stress that we let take over our lives. On a poster that hangs on the back of my door is a girl sitting on a beach chair. The quote paraphrases Psalm 46:10, "Chill, and know that He is God." I love that poster because of its daily reminder to me. If we take the time to stop, and let go of worry long enough to remember the Lord who is with us, we would have the wonderful experience of peace that our God gives to those who believe in Him. I stress a lot at times. It isn't until I take my worries and stresses to Him in prayer that I find peace. With that peace I find the answers and strength I need to meet the challenges of being a teenager.

Praise God for His wonderful gift to us. Don't let stress take control of your life. He has given us life and hope through His Son, Jesus. The Holy Spirit helps us to praise and glorify God.

Prayer: Dear heavenly Father, I thank You and praise You for being my refuge and strength in my times of need. Please help me keep You as the main focus in my life and remember You throughout my busy and stressful days. Be with me each and every day as I continue to live my life to Your glory. In Your name I pray. Amen.

The Game of Life

Read: Ephesians 6

Imagine! What if your life was like a video game? Think about it, in a way it is!

Before you can begin playing a video game, someone has to turn the game on. That's what God did for us through our Baptism. When we were dead in our sins and in our sinful nature, God made us alive with Christ. He forgave all our sins (Colossians 2:13).

Now the game begins! The game character faces many challenges. Usually these challenges are battles between good and evil. In the midst of these battles, different weapons are available for the character to use to defeat the enemy. Once the character is equipped with his weapons, he sets out to conquer his enemies as he fights to win the game. In our real life, God has equipped us with His full armor that allows us to face daily challenges. God's defensive and offensive armor gives us the ability to stand firm. He gives us the belt of truth and the breastplate of righteousness.

Our feet are fitted with the readiness that comes from the Gospel. God tells us to take up the shield of faith and the helmet of salvation. We've been given the sword of the Spirit, which is the Word of God, and we're told to pray (Ephesians 6). God's armor covers us from head to toe.

Of course, in reality the similarities of the video game character and our lives stop when the character fights the "final battle" to win the game. The video game character battles alone with only a few weapons, until "game over" flashes across the screen. We're different because we're not alone. We have the Savior, Jesus Christ. We're different because we have the Holy Spirit who was poured out on us generously through our Baptism and lives in us. We have the hope of eternal life (Titus 3:5–8). We're different because we have the full armor of God (Ephesians 6). We're different because we've been saved by grace, through faith. We're God's workmanship created in Jesus Christ (Ephesians 2:8–10). We're different because we don't have a "final battle" or "game over" in our lives because our game of life doesn't end. It begins with Jesus Christ.

Prayer: Lord, thank You for Your love and the way You have provided protection for me. I'm glad that You're in control of my life. Amen.

Soup or Salad?

Read: Luke 22:63–65; 23:35–37

As a tradition, my family always goes out to eat for each family member's birthday. I remember one particular dinner at The Olive Garden that turned out to be quite embarrassing. I told the waitress I wanted the parmesan chicken meal. She in turn asked me if I would like soup or salad and waited for a response. I quizzically looked around the table at my family. Finally my brother leaned over and said, "Ask her what the soup is." I looked up at the waitress and asked, "What's the super salad?" Then she gave me a curious look and said, "The soup of the day is . . ." Suddenly I understood what I had said. I could feel my face turning a deep red. My family found my mistake humorous and could not stop laughing. They had a reason to laugh . . . my blondness shone through.

Just imagine for a moment walking into a room full of people laughing. At first you think it is great, what a happy place. But then you realize they are all laughing at you. You have no idea why. What did you do? Is there someone behind you they are laughing at? No, well then, why are they laughing?

It is not fun being laughed at. Jesus was laughed at too. When we think of Good Friday and Jesus' crucifixion we commonly think of the physical torture Jesus suffered. But what about the hours before the crucifixion? Soldiers, kings, and others laughed and jeered at Jesus. They mocked Jesus and made fun of Him. Had He done anything to make others laugh? Had He mistaken the words "soup or salad" for "super salad"?

Although Jesus had the power to stop their laughter, He didn't. Out of love for you and me, Jesus suffered through the embarrassment and humiliation. Furthermore, He put on a crown of thorns, He was nailed to a cross, He died, and He rose from the dead. He is our Savior. Through faith in Jesus' death and resurrection we are set free from our burden of sin. We will live with Him forever because of His love and grace. We can rejoice in His love! Be happy—laugh—Jesus has saved us!

Prayer: Dear Lord, thanks for being laughed at for my sake. You were humiliated, beaten, bruised, and crucified for me. Thank You for Your amazing love! Thank You that I can live each day rejoicing in Your grace. In Your precious name. Amen.

Christ Our Cornerstone

Read: 1 Corinthians 3:10–11

What are you building on your foundation? What do you use as your foundation for living? As Christians, our foundation has been laid in the person of Jesus Christ. Even David, in his distress, acknowledges the foundation that God has built. He says, "In the beginning You laid the foundations of the earth, and the heavens are the work of Your hands"(Psalm 102:25). Not only did God lay these foundations, but He also laid us on the solid cornerstone of Jesus. Paul writes in Ephesians, "You are no longer foreigners and aliens, but fellow citizens with God's people and members of God's household, built on the foundation of the apostles and prophets, with Christ Jesus Himself as the chief cornerstone" (2:19–20).

We are children of God! Once we are established on this foundation, God instructs us how to build on this foundation through God's Word and the power of the Holy Spirit. God also

(Sarah Cusson

puts us into communities of faith with other believers. As we gather together to study God's Word, pray, and praise God's name, we grow in our faith. "Now it is God who makes both us and you stand firm in Christ. He anointed us, set His seal of ownership on us, and put His Spirit in our hearts as a deposit, guaranteeing what is to come" (2 Corinthians 1:21–22).

Prayer: Powerful, triune God, may we, by Your power, continue to be made strong daily as we study Your Word, make use of the Sacraments, and come to You in prayer. Help us to build our lives on the firm foundation of Jesus Christ. In His name we pray. Amen.

Give Thanks

Read: Psalm 63:4

Praising God seems easy enough to do, right? He blesses each and every one of us on a daily basis, yet how much do we show our appreciation by giving Him praise? I'd like you to think about it. How many times a week do you talk to our Father? Once a week in church each Sunday? Maybe twice a week, or when something goes wrong? That's not how it should be. God provides us with everything we have. Look around at the belongings you have. God provides you with forgiveness and life with Him. Look at the salvation you have.

In response to the gift of salvation that is ours through faith, we should honor God. There are so many different ways to extol God. For example, singing! Even if you may not think your voice is great, you can still read the words to praise God. Even reading poems and stories that reflect your faith is a way to praise God and demonstrate to others who you are and what you believe in. Even praying and talking to God is a way to thank Him.

Maybe you have a talent that you have not discovered yet. It's there. God has given every single one of us something unique as a gift. Whatever your gift, God gave it to you. We show Him our gratitude by giving something back. We can use God's gifts for His good as we use these talents to benefit the church and others around us.

God not only gives us all things that we need, He also provides opportunities to give Him thanks. Through your participation in the worship service, and your service to others, you speak of the wonderful gift of faith given to you by our heavenly Father.

Prayer: Lord God, thank You for everything You've done in our lives; You give us everything in our lives whether we realize it or not. Bless us and keep us strong in our faith so we can continue to praise You all our lives. Guide our ways and help us to share Your Word with everyone we can. Let it be, Father. In Your name. Amen.

You Feed Them

Read: John 6:1–13

Some of my teachers love giving tests; they just make me nervous. Pop quizzes are even worse. But did you realize that even Jesus gave "pop quizzes" to His disciples? In John 6 Jesus and His disciples were surrounded by 5,000 hungry men, plus women and children. Jesus asks Philip, "Where shall we buy bread for all these people to eat?" John adds that Jesus asks this question only to test him, for Jesus already had in mind what He was going to do.

Sometimes it seems like Jesus asks us to do something that we cannot do. In Luke's account of the feeding of the 5,000 Jesus tells His disciples, "You give them something to eat" (Luke 9:13). Now there's an impossible test to pass! With Philip we would respond, "Eight months' wages would not buy enough bread for each one to have a bite" (John 6:7) or, "Are you talking to me, God?"

Like the disciples we see the physical needs of those around us. They may need food, shelter, or other basics of daily life. But what they need most of all is the same thing the crowd of 5,000+ needed—they need a Savior. Jesus' disciples didn't understand that His direction that they should feed the people wasn't referring to just their physical need for food, but also to their spiritual need for salvation. Through the power of God's Spirit at Pentecost, the disciples were equipped to carry out the work of feeding the hungry souls throughout the world.

You and I get to participate in that task. God gives us His Word and Sacraments and strengthens us to share the news of Jesus with others. In all that you do you have the opportunity to share God's message of salvation with others. What do we have to offer Jesus in the way of resources? Probably just 5 loaves and 2 fish . . . But when we put what we have in His hands, it will be more than enough . . . and there will be leftovers.

Prayer: Heavenly Father, sometimes the task before me looks impossible. Strengthen me. In faith let me trust in You. Help me to be ready and willing to share Your Word when the opportunity arrives. In Jesus' name. Amen.

Live

I long for Your salvation, O LORD, and Your law is my delight. Let me live that I may praise You, and may Your laws sustain me.

Psalm 119:174-175

Living Out Loud!

Read: Matthew 5:14–16

In his song "Live Out Loud" Steven Curtis Chapman sings about how a Christian's faith is expressed in their life. I think this is just what we are called by God to do, LIVE OUT LOUD! You may be thinking, what exactly does this mean?

God calls each one of us to live out what we say we believe each and every day through the things that we do. Living out our love for Jesus doesn't mean just wearing a cross necklace to school and going to church on Sundays. Living for Christ allows others to see Jesus in us.

God is our Creator and He wants every person to come to know Him as Lord and Savior. This happens as we witness to our faith in Christ through our lives. We must reach out to people who don't know Christ as Lord and Savior from sin and Satan. We don't have to go to the other side of the world to reach out, we can do this every day by how we live.

But we can never do this on our own. We must rely completely on the power of God's Spirit, which was given to us at our Baptism. We can depend on the Spirit to strengthen our faith through our study of God's Word and participating in the Sacrament of Holy Communion.

Being a Christian and LIVING OUT LOUD for Christ is never easy. Jesus makes this clear to us in 2 Timothy 1:12. As Christians, you and I will face suffering and trials of many kinds. We might be hurt spiritually, emotionally, or even physically by people who think we are weird because of the way we live and what we believe. Even during these hard times, Christ tells us to never get tired of doing good (2 Thessalonians 3:13).

Even though LIVING OUT LOUD for God seems tough, you and I can put our trust in Christ and He will always be there to guide us along the right path. Even when LIVING OUT LOUD seems impossible, it's possible. Everything is possible when we have God on our side.

Prayer: Father, I thank You so much for Your awesome love. I pray that You would be with me today and every day, helping me to LIVE OUT LOUD for You so that others might come to know You. Father, I pray that people might see You in me through what I say and do. Thank You for sending Your Son to pay for our sins. I love You, Lord. Amen.

Freely Give

Shaina Erwin

106

Read: Luke 12:13–21;
1 Corinthians 5:11–21

Tomas went to church every week. He never missed a Sunday. When it was time to gather the offering, he gave nothing. Tomas wanted to keep the money for himself and not offer it up to God. One night Tomas read the parable of the rich fool (Luke 12) and realized that this story in Scripture was talking about him. He realized his sin and felt bad. The next Sunday Tomas went to church and gave a generous offering. When Tomas realized that God was the source of all that he had, he wanted to share his wealth.

We all fall victim to the sin of selfishness, but Jesus died for all our sins in the most selfless act ever. 2 Corinthians 5:15 says, "And He died for all, that those who live should no longer live for themselves, but for Him who died for them and was raised again." Christ loved us unto death. As His children we live for Him and not for ourselves. Tomas offered his earnings to God since he realized they were already God's. As we grow in our faith Christ enables us to live for Him and not for ourselves.

Prayer: God, we bow down our heads today to pray for forgiveness for our selfishness. Help us to share the gifts You have given us with others. Allow us to live for You and show Your love to the world. Amen.

It's a Different World

Read: Romans 12:14–21

Bob had just moved to Little Rock from California, and he didn't like it. His parents were pretty wealthy and his dad got transferred. He always got everything he wanted. His parents picked out a high school for him to go to, and he pitched a hissy-fit about it. He went to the school and came home the first day with a black eye and an in-school suspension note. His parents asked what happened and he said, "That school is dumb and the kids are stupid and they talk funny." His parents grounded him and said that he shouldn't judge people by the way they talk.

His dad said, "The South is a different culture, Bob. You wouldn't make fun of British people, would you?"

Romans 12:16 says, "Live in harmony with one another. Do not be proud, but be willing to associate with people of low position. Do not be conceited." People judge people by the way they look and talk. This keeps us from living in harmony with others. All we need to do is start out by saying a few kind words and treating others with respect.

If you read the verses from Romans 12 you know how difficult that list of "to do's" is. By ourselves it is impossible. It is only through the power that God gives us through His Word and the Sacraments that we can begin to do the things that He tells us to do. Further, when we fail to do these things, God forgives us through the blood of Jesus shed at Calvary.

Prayer: Dear God, please be with us throughout the day and help us to be kind to others and see what's on the inside. Thank You for sending Your Son to die for us. In Jesus' name. Amen.

Alive in Christ

Read: Romans 6:1–14

What are you living for? So often our lives become so busy and cluttered up with school, work, sports, music, and so many activities that we become overwhelmed and wander about aimlessly. We often neglect spending time with God and lose focus in the sinful world around us. Does life become so comfortable that only when we hurt we turn to God asking for quick help? Thankfully our Lord Jesus Christ is always there and will indeed offer that quick help when we need it, but He wants to have a loving relationship with us and for us to make Him our life—our whole life.

Unfortunately, Satan tries extremely hard to distract Christians from life in and with Christ. St. Paul asks Christians, "We died to sin; how can we live in it any longer?" The truth is we no longer need to live in our sin, for Christ Jesus has conquered death and the devil with His death and resurrection. We can therefore live confidently in our Lord and through Him and His strength serve as an "instrument of righteousness."

God has poured His Spirit upon us, which we as believers have received in our Baptism. How awesome it is that through our Baptism we belong to God and the family of believers. Look around you today and notice the large family of believers. Isn't it great to have so many brothers and sisters in Christ!

Our Baptism marks the beginning of our life with God; heaven awaits us after our death. But what is our purpose as Christians? St. Paul encourages us to live as a people *alive* in Christ and joyful in that promise. Our time on earth may be temporary, but we have a mission as a body of believers to reach out and show the love of Christ and share the Gospel of our Lord. The parting words of Jesus in Matthew 28 outline our purpose and our mission: "Therefore go and make disciples of all nations, baptizing them in the name of the Father and of the Son and of the Holy Spirit, and teaching them to obey everything I have commanded you. And surely I am with you always, to the very end of the age." That's our mission; but don't worry, we do not need to go out on our own. The Holy Spirit is working through us as we share the Gospel in our world to bring believers to Christ.

As sinful and imperfect creatures, we will undoubtedly fall short of God's law, but despite all our failings, Jesus Christ is there to pick us up and carry us with His forgiveness. What an awesome promise! Rest assuredly in the Lord's promise that "we too may live a new life" though our Lord and Savior Jesus Christ

Live confidently in your Baptism and live *ALIVE in CHRIST!!!*

Prayer: Heavenly Father, thank You for my Baptism and my brothers and sisters in Christ. May You pour out Your Holy Spirit upon me so that I may be *alive in Christ* and filled with a passion to share Christ's love with others. Amen.

Walking by Faith

Read: Matthew 14:22–32

What is faith? Faith is a gift of God. It is the means by which we relate to God and live our lives in freedom without fear of sinking.

In these passages from Matthew we see Peter exercising faith in Jesus by stepping out of the boat to walk on water. We also see what happens to Peter when he saw the wind and was afraid. He took his focus off of Jesus and began to sink because his circumstances became greater than his faith.

Sometimes we are a lot like Peter and our focus is not on Christ but on our circumstances. Like Peter we have enough faith to get out of the boat, but we are not strong enough in our faith to stand up to a storm.

But all is not lost.

What happens to Peter next? Does he sink to the bottom of the lake? No, he cried out and said, "Lord, save me." Immediately Jesus reached out His hand and caught him.

Jesus does the same thing for each of us.

Jesus takes hold of us each time we read the Word of God. God's Word says that "We [live] by faith, not by sight" (2 Corinthians 5:7). "Without faith, it is impossible to please [God]," (Hebrews 11:6) and, finally, "faith comes from hearing, and hearing through the word of Christ" (Romans 10:17).

Faith in Jesus is what helps us to get through all things in life. In faith we know that God is always there for us, no matter what. Although we may sin and fail along the way, God continues to reach out His hand and pick us up. The devil and the world may cause us to focus on the storms around us and it may take us awhile to realize we are sinking, but we can be confident that Jesus is right there with His hand out-stretched. He lifts us up out of the darkness and gives us comfort and protection. Through faith in Jesus Christ we can never be too far away from God's helping hand.

Prayer: Dear Jesus, help me to fix my eyes on You and not on the storms in life. Help me to live by faith and not by sight. May Your Word guide and strengthen me in all circumstances. Amen.

Leap of Faith

Read: Jeremiah 1:5–8

"Why did I have to do it? There had to be people more qualified than me to go serve. Besides, I had never even been out of the country, except to visit relatives living in Canada. I didn't even know where Haiti was, but I knew it was beyond the imagination of a Chicago girl like myself."

This all started six months ago. I was visiting my grandparents for the holiday. Like a good granddaughter, I was up bright and early to go to church with them on Sunday. At church, I was approached by a smiling lady who struck up a conversation with me. She was recruiting youth for a mission trip to Haiti. Not even five minutes into the conversation she turns to me and says, "You will come with us, right?"

So, six months later I found myself loading a bus bound for the airport with 13 complete strangers. It was hard to suppress the tears that yearned to flow as I hugged everyone I knew and said goodbye. With my knees wobbling and my heart pounding, I stepped onto the bus and took a seat in the back. I prayed hard and fast those first few hours of the trip. I prayed for strength. I prayed for companionship. I prayed for God's will to be done.

By the time I boarded the plane my outlook on life had changed. No longer was there fear or anxiety; instead, I felt excited—at peace. I was surrounded by brothers and sisters in Christ. We spent ten days in Haiti building a church, teaching, providing healthcare, and ministering to people less fortunate than I could have possibly imagined.

God opened a door of service opportunity for me, and He blessed me. In Jeremiah 1:7–8 the Lord says, "Do not say, 'I am only a child.' You must go to everyone I send you to and say whatever I command you. Do not be afraid of them, for I am with you and will rescue you." Where is God calling you? How has God opened doors for you? Have you been able to take that leap of faith? What is holding you back? God provides the opportunities, calms our fears, and gives us His Spirit so we can do all that He commands.

Prayer: Dear Father, I pray that You will send me the opportunities to follow Your calling. Help calm my fears, and grant me Your guidance with each new opportunity. Give me dreams for the future and strength to take that leap of faith. In Jesus' name. Amen

Perfect Rules

Read: Psalm 19:7–8

I've noticed that, as teens, we seem to have a larger number of rules hanging over our heads than any other age group. Not only are we under federal law and parental law, but we're also under God's Law. It's no wonder many of us are frustrated, stressed, and disobedient.

But why? That's what I always wondered. Why us? Why aren't we respected? Why aren't we acknowledged?

Sometimes rules can be difficult to understand. We often use words like "unfair, ridiculous, and stupid" to describe them. Although I'm sure we all know why rules exist, we still resent the fact that "rules are rules" and we have to abide by them. This kind of attitude tends to fire up our sinful nature, eventually steering us onto a rebellious road.

While the rules set forth by mankind are important, what we really need to be focused on are the rules set forth by God. These rules are the ones that we can always trust. They are relevant to every situation. There are never any gray areas. God really does know what's best for us, so He restricts us accordingly. Our sinful nature makes it impossible to keep God's rules. We fail. And that failure is ours, not any shortcoming or error in God's Law. Yet it is when we fail that God shows us His mercy, for in our failure we realize that we can't do it on our own, and we see the need for our Savior, Jesus.

Our Lord kept all of the rules perfectly. He's the only one who could, because He is God. Then He allowed Himself to be crucified, punished in our place. Three days later He rose again from the dead to guarantee our eternal life with Himself in heaven.

God still loves us when we fail. He still loves us when we fight, when we curse, and even when we push Him away. He always loves us, and He always wants to help us. So when we feel like His rules are unfair, ridiculous, or stupid, He loves us, He forgives us and covers our failures with His love.

Prayer: Dear Jesus, thank You so much for Your unconditional love. Thank You for picking us up when we fall and giving us another chance. Please help us to remember that You know all, and You see all. You know what we need, and You see our hearts. Help us to better understand Your Word, so that we can follow close to You. Hold out Your hand to us, Lord, so that we don't lose sight of Your footsteps. Speak clearly to us; show us what to do, and keep us safe. Jesus Christ, in Your holy name we pray. Amen.

A Reluctant Servant

Read: Luke 7:11–17

Last spring break my parents signed me up to go with our church youth group on a mission trip to Mexico for five days. I already had plans to hang out with my friends all break. I was really mad when my parents told me I had no choice but to go. Besides the fact that I wouldn't know anyone, I hated the thought of being stuck in a foreign country doing nothing but building houses and feeding dirty homeless people. I was thinking about running away to a friend's house until the bus left, but that was a little childish. Already 10 minutes late, I packed a bag of clothes and left for church.

I was surprised to discover that after the first day in Mexico I was having so much fun. It turns out I knew one girl on the trip who went to my elementary school. We were pretty close the whole trip. I met lots of other people too. Seven of us spent three days helping build a house for a large family. It felt really good knowing I had done something that would actually make a difference in someone's life. But the thing that touched me the most was when we all went to an orphanage. I visited with kids ages 3–12. All of them were so thankful to God that He had given them the life they had. They were so happy with the little they had and the "fiesta food" they had (which was not a lot). To them it was a huge amount of food. I felt really sad when this blond-haired, blue-eyed boy came up to me and asked me (in Spanish) if I was his mother (I have blonde hair and blue eyes too!).

I thought my trip to Mexico was going to be horrible, but in the end, it turned out completely the opposite. God used this experience to help me grow up and appreciate the things I have. I'm glad He did.

The story of the widow's son (Luke 7:11–15) reminds us of Jesus' compassion for a woman He did not know. He saw the despair of the woman and, without being asked, brought her dead son back to life. Deserved or undeserved, asked for or ignored, Jesus came to live and die for us to show His love to all. Through Him we receive faith, forgiveness, and eternal life.

Prayer: Heavenly Father, just as through Christ You showed Your mercy to the widow and her son, help us to share Your mercy with others. Use us to carry out Your work in our world. In Jesus' name. Amen.

A Dying Wish

Read: Colossians 1:9–14

A few years ago, my father was diagnosed with a terminal disease. The doctors told him he had about one year to live. At that time my sister and I were under split custody between my mother and father. My father decided that he should try to take us away from the poor care we were receiving at our mother's house. He filed a court case against my mother in family court to gain full custody, on the grounds that my sister and I were receiving inadequate care.

A year passed, and my father was still quite alive. The court battles were still going on. Every time there was a hearing my father would stand up, despite the pain it would cause him, and talk to the judge. When the court case was finally settled, Dad set about giving my grandparents guardianship. He made them the ones who would take over custody of my sister and me when he passed away. Almost immediately after he got that settled, Dad's condition started getting worse.

My father hadn't been a religious man for most of the time I knew him, but after being diagnosed I noticed him reading the Bible and devotional books. When my dad finally died, he had a peace that couldn't be matched by anything on this earth.

At that time I wasn't a religious person at all, but now I understand that the strength of Christ gave my father the ability to finish his business on earth. By faith my father knew that when his final hour came, his heavenly Father would be there to bring him to his eternal home in heaven.

Prayer: Heavenly Father, help me to trust in You alone. Keep me from the things that distract me from You. Through Your Word and Sacraments, strengthen me in my faith every day. In Your name I pray. Amen.

Too Young

Read: 1 Timothy 4:12

I am sure you've been told that you are too young to do that or have to be a certain age to do this. For example, in most states you cannot drive until you are 16. Age always seems to be a limitation. In God's eyes, we can always be a testimony for Him. He calls us, regardless of our age, to be examples for believers and unbelievers. Even if you are too young to teach a Sunday school class or to go on a mission trip, your actions are a witness every day. Others look at you and wonder what you have that makes you so different, and some may even ask questions about the hope that you have. This gives you the opportunity to be a witness and to tell others about your faith in Christ.

As Christians, we need to remember that people are watching us. Our actions say a lot about us, and our God. This "always being on display" puts an extra strain on young Christians. People in our world expect us be on our best behavior at all times. Our God knows that we are not perfect. That is why He sent Jesus to earn our forgiveness through His suffering and death. God forgives us when we fail. His Spirit helps us live a life of witness for Him.

Prayer: Lord God, I thank You for Your unconditional love. Even when others look down on me, You stay closer than a brother. I pray that You would give me the strength to keep going even when other people look down on me. Reassure me that You are with me. Give me strength to keep going when others try to bring me down. I pray this in Your Son's holy name. Amen.

Plans

Read: Jeremiah 29:11

I often think about my future. I have spent hours in front of my computer, researching what I think is my perfect college. I know exactly where I'll apply, what I'll write in my application essay, and when I'll move into my dorm room. But what if God's plan isn't the same as my own?

I love to look at maps. There is a map of the world in our kitchen at home. I often stand in front of it and plan exactly where I think our family should go during our summer vacation. I research the best route to get to our destination. I could tell you the best "tourist traps" between here and there. I know exactly how we should get there and what we should do. But what if God's plan isn't the same as my own?

Sometimes when I'm at the bookstore, I read through all of the bridal magazines. By now I know exactly when I will be getting married, what my wedding dress will look like, what kind of flowers I'll be holding, and what kind of food will be served at the reception. But what if God's plan isn't the same as my own? What if He wants me to serve Him as a single person?

Recently I've begun to learn the answer to the "What if?" questions. What if God's plans differ from my plans? Romans 8:28 says, "And we know that in all things God works for the good of those who love Him, who have been called according to His purpose." God has a perfect plan for my life, a plan which surpasses my wildest imagination. God loves each and every one of His followers, including myself, so much that He has the best possible plan for each and every one of our lives—the plan for our salvation! While my plans may work out, God's plan is sure and certain. Through Jesus Christ God's plan for everlasting life with Him in His kingdom is complete.

For now, I continue to daydream about my future. God has given me my reason and intelligence to make decisions about my life. Strengthened by the Holy Spirit, I can be confident in the plans I make— they will either be used by Him, or forgiven by Him. I can look forward to seeing where my future and the future of other believers lead as we live according to God's plan.

Prayer: Dear Lord, help me to continue to realize how much You love me. Help me to realize that because of Your love, You have the very best plan for my life. I know You will do what is best for me. Please lead me according to Your perfect plan. In Your name I pray. Amen.

Running for the Prize

Read: 1 Corinthians 9:24–25

"Do you not know that in a race, all runners run, but one gets the prize? Run in such a way as to get the prize" (1 Corinthians 9:24). As a cross-country runner this verse seems quite reasonable. Whenever running in a race, the ultimate goal is to get first place. I don't run to get second or third place. My mind is set on what it takes to be first.

As Christians we understand that St. Paul is speaking of the race that is our daily life. We "run" or go through our daily lives to receive the ultimate prize, which is eternal life in heaven. Being a long distance cross-country runner, I see the race that Paul talks about as a long-distance race, not a sprint. It is a hard, long journey against the competition, the devil, who tries to throw Christians off course. In verse 25 Paul reminds us, "They do it to get a crown that will not last; but we do it to get a crown that will last forever." The prize in this race is eternal life in paradise with our Savior, Jesus Christ. The people who go for "the crown that will not last" are the people that just "run" for earthly pleasure and possessions.

No one ever said that running a good, strong race would be easy. Just as a runner must train for upcoming races, we stay in training for our "race" by attending church, participating in Bible study, and receiving Christ's body and blood in Holy Communion. This is how we stay "in shape." God gives us these gifts to strengthen us for our daily race.

Another important part of our race is to spread the Word of Jesus to other runners. In Acts 20:24 it says, "I consider my life worth nothing to me, if only I may finish the race and complete the task the Lord Jesus has given me—the task of testifying to the gospel of God's grace." The life that God has graciously given us prepares us to do all those things which are necessary and pleasing in God's sight. This means to take the gospel of salvation through faith in Jesus Christ to all who need to hear it.

In a race there are tough stretches, with many hills or rough terrain, as well as the pain that comes with the race. We go through stretches where we face much pain and temptations. The pain we face daily can either be temporary or long lasting. But Jesus has given us the promise of eternal life with Him, and He assures us we have nothing in this life to worry about. Our Savior is running right with us. But at the same time, Jesus has already completed the race. He ran it perfectly and completely and finished it with His suffering, death, and resurrection. Because of Him, we can run knowing that He has already run the race for us.

Prayer: Dear Lord, help me run a race that is pleasing in Your sight. Let me take comfort in knowing that You have already run the race and that You are always running with us. Amen.

Tough Decisions

Read: James 1:5

Are you facing a tough decision and the answer isn't obvious? Maybe you're trying to decide which college to attend. Or maybe a friend wants you to do something.

I recently had to make a tough decision in my life. I was a football player. Did you notice I used the word "was"? I played football my first three years in high school. The summer before my senior year I trained six days a week. I was in the best physical condition of my life. I began the season with the expectation that I would be a starter. I was strong. I was fast. I worked hard in practice. I was a senior. I wanted to play.

However, something happened the day before the first game. I looked at the game day sheet and there I was third-string offense and second-string defense as a senior. The coaches were starting a sophomore and a junior before me. What happened? What were they thinking? How embarrassing! At that point I knew I had one of those tough decisions to make. What should I do? I needed to pray for wisdom (James 1:5). I needed to go to God's Word for guidance (Psalm 110:105).

That night my parents and I prayed and read God's Word. I asked God for the strength to use the gifts He had given me, my reason, my senses, and my intelligence, to make wise choices regarding football.

The next night at the first football game, I stood on the sidelines watching the clock tick down in the fourth quarter to 28 seconds. I heard my name. I ran onto the field. I played less than 10 seconds. The game was over. What a disappointment! In my heart I had planned a course regarding football, but that night the Lord determined my steps (Proverbs 16:9). I saw the power of prayer in action. The answer to my tough decision was obvious. Football was over.

The next day I had to tell the head coach that I was leaving the team. This was a difficult task. I was leaving something behind for which I had worked hard. I asked God to help guide my words and actions when I talked to the coach. I had to trust in the Lord and not lean on my own understanding (Proverbs 3:5-6).

I have to say that I am convinced that prayer is vital in decision-making. I still don't understand why the coaches didn't play me, but that's okay. What I understand through this experience is that God strengthens His children for all the decisions we have to make in our lives. As believers we know the will of God for our lives. Yet in prayer we can approach Him with all the cares and concerns, knowing that He hears and cares. Strengthened with the Gospel reality that our whole life has been redeemed, even our choices, we hear in His Word the comfort and strength to make decisions.

Prayer: Lord, thank You for the wisdom You give me through Your Word. Help me trust in You for guidance in all things, for Your way is perfect. Amen.

Decision Time

Read: Psalm 119:25–27

For the last three years I have been battling with what to do in my future and the plans God has set before me. Like me, many other teens may be facing these same struggles. One of the biggest issues older teens face is deciding where to go to college. Some want to go as far away as possible. Others say they want to stay close to home, or go to college where their friends are going.

These can be the scariest times of a teen's life, waiting for the acceptance letter for the college they want to get into. It is harder yet to accept that not getting into "the school" is not the end of the world. God promises that He is with us and that we can put our trust in Him to help us and guide us as we make major decisions.

God has shown us His will for our life. It begins at Baptism and extends until we are forever with Him in heaven. Along the way we have decisions to make. Jesus calls this the narrow path, the path of faith.

Sometimes we may fall off that path, but He is always there to pick us up, dust us off, and put us back on the faithful way.

As we make decisions and pray about them, things begin to fall into place. Tough decisions will still face us throughout life, but having an understanding of what Jesus has done to secure our place with Him in eternity makes it a lot easier to make a decision. No matter how our futures turn out, or what decision we make, God's forgiving love keeps and protects us.

Prayer: Dear Father, please help me and guide me in my life to do what pleases You. I may stumble and fall off the path You have set before me, but I know You will be there to pick me up, dust me off, and set me back on it. In Your name I pray. Amen.

Living Hope

Read: 1 Peter 3:13–18

Have you ever wondered why you can't be the best at something? Why is there always someone better than you? Why do others think you are different because of the way you look? I realize that I do not have to look the best in my class, I do not have to be the smartest kid in the class. All that matters in my life is God.

God makes each one of us different. You may not be the star point guard, or the best setter on your volleyball team, but that is okay. God created you, molded you into who you are today. God does not look at the outside with how much make-up you put on your face or how much muscle you have. God knows us inside and out. He knows our hearts. He loves us because He knows the faith that is in our hearts.

The best compliment someone can ever get is another asking, "Are you a Christian? Because I can see it in your face." It is awesome how your faith can reflect through your actions.

God can show anyone who looks at you how much you love Him, and how much He loves you. This is your chance to witness the hope that you have in Christ.

You do not have to go out like Martin Luther and nail questions to a church door, or even talk to some person you do not know on the street. Little things like a smile to someone you do not know can brighten their day whether you know it or not. However, make sure you are ready if someone does in fact ask you about your faith. Be able to show them what you believe, and that it is true.

Remember, never be disappointed with who you are. God formed you to be *you*, not someone you think is a perfect person. God controls our life. All the twists and turns we go though, God is beside us the entire time. He keeps us safely within His nail-scarred hands.

Prayer: Lord, we come before You today focusing on one thing. We ask You to keep our faith with You. Remind us that we do not have to be the best at anything. All we need is to trust and believe in You, God. You save us. Thank You for always being there for us, whether we know it or not. Let it be so, Lord. Amen.

Shining Lights

Read: Matthew 5:16

Matthew 5:16 has become very important to me personally in two ways. For one, it is my confirmation verse, and secondly it reminds me of how God wants us to act.

Now I'm the first one to admit that I'm a lowly sinner. I do some regrettable things. I have the privilege of attending a Christian high school. There are times when I am out with my friends, wearing my school shirt, that I wonder what people think of me, and my actions. They probably think to themselves: "Look how those kids are acting. That's not how I think a Christian should act; I'm not going to do anything like that."

Sad to say, that's probably what most people think when they see Christians doing unpleasing actions. If I weren't a Christian and saw "Christians" doing stupid and foolish things, I would be turned off to the whole going to church idea. In fact, the most regrettable thing of all that is our actions could prevent those people from attending church or learning more about what we believe in.

Most people are under the impression that God saves us because of our good works. Sadly, even our best actions are not good enough. The free gift of faith in our Savior, Jesus Christ, is how we gain eternal life in heaven.

Good works are still necessary, they just aren't necessary for salvation. Our good works are the result of faith; it is only through faith in Jesus that our works become "good." Good works are important. Matthew 5:16 reminds us that not only do our good deeds show our respect for our Father in heaven, but when others see our good actions they will praise God as well.

In science class we learned that the moon doesn't generate its own light, but reflects the light of the sun. In the same way, we have no light of our own, but we can reflect the light of Christ. Through my actions I can let my— Christ's—light shine before other people.

Prayer: Dear Lord, thank You for the incredible gift of faith that You have given me through my Baptism. Help me act according to Your will. Let me bring glory to Your name through my actions. In Your name I pray. Amen.

You Make Me Sick!

Read: Proverbs 26:11

Think about the last thing you ate. What was it? Was it a hamburger, some cereal, cookies, maybe a steak? Imagine it was your favorite food. Now imagine that you suddenly vomit it up. Of course you would be disgusted, but would you later forget that you threw it up and come back to eat it? No way, right? However, I am sure you have all seen a dog do this at some time or another. Why don't humans do this? The dogs certainly seem to enjoy the meal the second time around.

By now you are probably wondering why I'm writing about eating your own vomit. If you read Proverbs 26:11 you may wonder why God felt that the digestive habits of dogs were important enough to write down in the Holy Scriptures. The answer is that when it comes to our sin, we act just like the dogs eating things they have vomited up. Every day we sin. We repent of our sins and ask God to forgive us. Thus we "throw up" our sins to God. It is no longer in us. But all too often we come right back, having forgotten how sorry we were about the sin in the first place, and gobble it up again. Seeing His children doing this disgusts God just as much as seeing our family pet eating the hamburger he ate an hour ago for the second time disgusts us.

Now after your dog re-eats the hamburger, are you going to rush right over and pet him and let him lick your face? No, probably not, because you are sickened by his habits and his lack of memory. God, however, comes right over and helps us spiritually wipe off our mouths. He loves us no matter how much our repetitive sins disgust Him.

You may think that we aren't nearly as forgetful as the dogs are, but remember the children of Israel in the wilderness. As you read the Bible, it seems that in every other chapter they fall away from God. In the next chapter something bad happens and they run back to God and repent. As soon as things start going well, they fall away again. You might think that you are better than the Israelites. After all, your attention span is longer than 5 minutes. The reality is that it's easier to see others' sin rather than our own. But the good news is that no matter how often we fail God, He freely offers us forgiveness through His Son, Jesus.

Prayer: Dear God, thank You for always being there for me even though my sins disgust You. Help me to always turn to You in true repentance. Keep me from returning to my sin through the power of Your Spirit. In the name of Jesus my Savior. Amen.

An Unfogged Future

Read: Isaiah 42:16

It all begins with the age-old question, "What am I going to be when I grow up?" Few of us can actually answer this question during our young teen years. But think about it—we all want to know where we are going in life and what God's will is for us. We sometimes wish God would spell out His plan for us in huge block letters or write it across the sky or broadcast it from some heavenly loudspeaker.

It's very easy for us to want to see our lives unfolded before us so that we can have assurance and satisfaction that what we see *will* come true. God knows our future. He knows every problem we will go through, the people that will come into our lives, our achievements, our failures, our mistakes. But here's the twist: God does not tell us our future. Because despite how wonderful it would be to see an outline of our future, it's going to be even more wonderful to experience every moment of our lives firsthand and unexpectedly. God has great things planned for us, and He assures of this in His Word. Jeremiah 29:11 tells us, "'For I know the plans I have for you,' declares the LORD, 'plans to prosper you and not to harm you, plans to give you hope and a future.'"

But God's greatest plan for you is eternal life with Him in heaven. So plan and dream for the future and reach for them. Put your trust in God and He will not only hold you in His hands, but lift you up so that you can reach your dream.

Prayer: Most merciful God, order my life so that I may know what You want me to do, and then help me to do it. Help me to put my complete trust in You, so that I can have the satisfaction of a bright future with You. When I become scared or unsure of what lies ahead, lift me up so that I can see Your will. And as I rely on You, let my faith be an example to others of how amazing Your love is. All these things I ask in Your name. Amen.